A

MONKEY

COULD DO

YOUR JOB

A

Practical Tactics

MONKEY

for Understanding and Overcoming

COULD DO

Crazy Feelings about Work

YOUR JOB

FRAZER BUNTIN

BOOKLOGIX˙
Alpharetta, GA

ISBN: 978-1-61005-952-7
eISBN: 978-1-61005-953-4
eISBN: 978-1-61005-954-1

Library of Congress Control Number: 2018915285

Printed in the United States of America   021819

⊗This paper meets the requirements of ANSI/NISO Z39.48-1992
(Permanence of Paper)

*For Tiffany, who cheered me on throughout my career,
listened to me deal with the monkey times,
and helped me find the last chapter.
I love you so much.*

Life occurs in the gray areas.

CONTENTS

PREFACE
I FEEL LIKE WRITING A BOOK

(Let me know when you're done whether it was helpful.)

Frazer,

I just wanted to thank you for an awesome training session today. I'm early in my career and have read many books, articles, etc. on career development in the past year. I have to tell you that your story, advice, and graphics resonated with me more than any articles out there. I know you joked about the slides not being copyrighted, but you could certainly author a compelling novel—and heck, you already have a catchy title!

Really appreciate your time and advice. I hope you have a safe trip back to Nashville.

Best,
Julianne

That was it. That simple email was the catalyst to get me started writing this book.

It was sent from a colleague of mine after a presentation I had given on career development, titled "From Toilet Paper to

CEO: A Wandering but Deliberate Approach to Professional Development." This was most definitely not the title our human resources department gave me when they asked me to make the presentation, but after reflecting on my professional journey and all the crazy-ass experiences it entailed, I thought it would get people to the event. Thanks, human resources, for humoring me.

Let me start by saying that I have indeed had some crazy-ass professional experiences, as many people have. Those experiences have allowed me to learn valuable lessons about work and life, which I share with you in this book. But more important than the lessons themselves is the context surrounding those lessons. By *context*, I mean the feelings we have during these types of experiences. The feelings are what prove most revealing. This book gives voice to how we feel at different times in our careers and why it's okay to feel that way, along with practical tactics for what to do about it.

Feelings are an inherent part of being human. It's our feelings that drive us to stress out. It's our feelings that cause us to stay up late. It's our feelings that get us pumped about life. Though feelings drive so much of our lives, in the professional world we get little to no context for these feelings and even less direction on what to do about them. We don't want to admit how we feel to our bosses or colleagues. And if we do get up the guts to talk to our bosses about our emotions, most of them are not qualified to respond in a productive manner. Addressing this friction as individuals is important to our contentment, so yes, you are holding a book about professional feelings.

I use this framework because within our feelings is the *context* for the intense questions and challenges we face in our professional lives. Humans are curious, and we work and live and exist more effectively when we have context and understanding. Understanding the context helps us understand the "why," which in turn helps us work (and live) more effectively. When we understand the why, we can actually go about solving problems, addressing challenges, and making decisions. To help with the context, I give specific tactics not only for understanding our feelings but also for doing something productive about them.

I have found that there are common sets of feelings across almost all jobs and industries for all people, regardless of age or gender. The same ones have shown up in meeting after meeting throughout my career. They are:

> ➢ "I feel overwhelmed."
> ➢ "I feel bored."
> ➢ "I feel stuck."
> ➢ "I'm not excited anymore."

And many others in this same genre. You may notice that all these feelings have a negative connotation. I reference negative feelings not to depress you but to help you confront the emotions that most confuse and concern us in our professional lives. We generally don't worry or have questions when our jobs are going well and our experiences are uplifting. The material in this book is for the people who are uncertain, struggling, lost, frustrated, discouraged—all that good stuff. I say "good" because we can use those feelings and our understanding of the origins of those feelings to bring about valuable change in our lives.

I should warn you that the way I write is reflective of the way we feel when we experience the questions, concerns, and anxieties that characterize certain stages in our careers. If an experience I had in the past made me feel like shit, I have written that it made me feel like shit. If an experience made me mad as hell, I have explained why it made me mad as hell. If your feelings are always G-rated, some parts of this book may not suit you. If you occasionally have feelings that are R-rated, then some of the language will resonate with you as well.

You may not have experienced all of the feelings or situations referenced in this book at the time you read it. My guess is at some point you probably will, and then you'll be glad you're prepared for it ahead of time. Understanding the context in advance will help you immensely when these situations do occur. And you can come back to different chapters, using them in a focused way to help you navigate certain situations. Consider the book a catchall for the full spectrum of career shit you might encounter.

For purposes of context, below is a chronology of my career to date. I don't share this chronology to imply success but rather to frame the stories I share throughout this book.

Age 22 – Graduate college from the University of the South (Sewanee)

Age 23 – Go to New Zealand and screw off for a year (highly recommend)

Age 24 – Logistics Planner, Dollar General Corporation

Age 25 – Supervisor of Logistics Planning, Dollar General

Age 26 – Associate Buyer of Cleaning and Paper Products, Dollar General

Age 28 – Director EZ Store Project, Dollar General

Age 30 – Senior Director Operations, Healthways Inc.

Age 33 – CEO and Co-Founder, Silvercare Solutions

Age 38 – CEO, White Glove Health

Age 39 – Market President, Evolent Health

Age 40 – Region President, Evolent Health

Age 41 – Solution President, Evolent Health
Age 42 – President, Value-Based Services, Evolent Health

Timelines are riveting, I know. Now, let's delve into the real stuff.

Top of the Funnel:

Feelings and Experiences
Early in Your Career

1
I Feel Like I Don't Know What I Am Meant to Do

I f you're like most people, you want a job that perfectly aligns with your passions and interests and skills. You want to leap out of bed and race to the office and be brilliant and passionate. You want to high-five your soul as you stand atop your career. You want to know with deep conviction that you are making the right decision. And you want "the answer" to come to you by divine inspiration. You feel the fragility of your career and you really do not want to mess it up. This is normal.

THE UNFOLDING OF YOUR CAREER

I remember vividly feeling this way early in my career, thinking there must be *one* specific industry that I had to get into to ensure I was on the "correct track" professionally. I made lists and considered each industry and had angst in my sleep at night and worried about taking the wrong job that could set me on the wrong path forever! I felt (and probably was) clueless. I didn't have an industry or career track that struck me as my one true passion or purpose. No matter how hard I felt I was looking, there didn't seem to be any clear answer for me.

You may also feel this way, and it's because you want to have some control over the process of the unfolding of your career. In much of the rest of your life, you have been able to make choices based on your preferences and you therefore assume that your preferences will guide your career. You feel this way because you don't want to miss out on all the rewarding experiences you think will come from a perfectly aligned career. This is absolutely normal. You have picked colleges, boyfriends and girlfriends, apartments, vacations, and many other parts of your life in this way. When you like something, it is relatively apparent to you, and you choose to go after that thing to make it part of your life. It would make sense that this is how career choices should work as well. The challenge, though, is that careers don't actually work this way for most of us. The scope of opportunity for professions is too large to digest or even begin to comprehend. But more importantly, it doesn't work that way because *there is no single right answer*. This truth is difficult. You want, maybe even expect, to find *the* perfect career for yourself.

I used to go back to the college I attended to participate in a career-development event for rising juniors and seniors. Each year, to address this point on career ambiguity, I did the same activity with the entire audience of several hundred students. I asked everyone to stand up. I then said that if you knew you wanted to be a doctor or you thought you were good enough to play professional sports, stay standing and everyone else could sit down. There were always a few future doctors who remained standing, as well as a few hopeful athletes. (I say hopeful because it was a Division III school.) The majority of the students, though, would be sitting, looking up nervously, casting envious glances at their classmates who were still on their feet. Why, at nineteen years old, were the students nervous or envious? The reason is that most of them had no firm answer to the unanswerable question that plagues so many people: "What do you want to do?"

I say this question is unanswerable because it assumes two things. The first assumption is that there is only one answer to the question. The second assumption is that the answer is static and remains the same over time.

> **Something I have learned:** The question "What do you want to do?" is not the right question.

A better question to ask yourself is "What could I do now that feels right?"

Consider that all of the students sitting in the audience, and even the ones remaining standing, were at the top of a professional and personal Funnel. The widest part of the Funnel. The students could do almost anything professionally and live almost anywhere in the world. They could seek a job on Wall Street or become a photographer in the mountains of Tibet. Yes, there would be logistics to contend with, but in essence the full spectrum of professional opportunities was available to them. Their careers had yet to enter the Funnel, which filters work opportunities through an ongoing Process of Elimination and Selection.

THE PROCESS OF ELIMINATION AND SELECTION

Early in my career, I worked as a resident real estate agent. I hated it. In fact, I disliked it so much, I left it off my career chronology in the preface of this book. I started doing it out of default, because I thought it would lead me into either residential development or historic renovation, both things I thought I might enjoy. The problem with being a real estate agent for me was the fact that the product I was selling was myself. Having myself as the product meant I had to do a lot of self-promotion. If you have ever gotten a business card from a residential realtor, you will know that many of them have the realtor's photograph on them. Why is it that no other industry does that?

The last straw came one night when I was showing property to a potential buyer. I don't actually think this guy had any money or any interest in buying a house but rather preyed on ignorant, starving, young realtors like me who would take any client they could get just in the hopes of facilitating a transaction. I met this guy on a weeknight on the outskirts of town in the parking lot of a grocery store. He got in my car so we could go look at a couple of different properties, and I noticed he was wearing a dirty T-shirt and jeans. Now, a smart realtor would have requested that he get prequalified for a mortgage loan before meeting him in the dark in a questionable part of town, but I was not a smart realtor. We had a list of houses to consider, which were all fairly rundown. On our way to the first house, it began to rain steadily. By the time we got there, the skies had opened up and it was dumping rain. The kind of rain that happens in the fall—cold and windy and thick. To get into the house, I had a little electronic device that I would insert into another device that was locked to the door handle of the house, which held the key. I told the guy to wait in the car while I went to get the key. I sprinted through the rain, inserted my device, and pressed the code that should have unlocked the key. Instead I got a series of three beeps telling me that my device needed payment to allow another three months of use. The fix was simple: I only needed to call the company and authorize another three months. However, this was 1998 and cell phones were literally the size of a brick, and battery life was not quite what it is today, so my phone was dead. We then had to drive to the nearest pay phone (yes, a pay phone—Google it) so I could stand in the driving rain on a pay phone to get the device updated so we could drive *back* to the creepy dark house on the edge of town. All the while, I was having to make small talk with dirty T-shirt guy. An hour later we finally got back to the house, unlocked the device, got the key, and did a walk-through of the place. Fast forward to 9:30 p.m., when we had seen three more houses in the pouring rain, and Dirty T-Shirt tells me he doesn't think he is ready to buy a house because none of the houses looked very nice. Damn you, Dirty T-Shirt!

There I was, pissed off and broke, ready to make some serious elimination decisions in my career Funnel. But that would also mean I had to make a selection. I knew I wanted to stay in Nashville but wanted to run as far from residential real estate as I could. I also knew I wanted to run as far away from jobs that require self-promotion and my face on a business card as I could. And I knew I wanted to select a job that was part of a company where employees work together instead of acting as independent contractors. I may have swung too far in my process of elimination. Perhaps if I had stuck with it, I would have discovered and enjoyed a different aspect of real estate, but regardless, I used the information I had at the time to make a change.

It is through this Process of Elimination and Selection that you slowly eliminate aspects of your career that you dislike or are not good at doing, and you select aspects of your career that you do like and are good at doing. If you choose Wall Street, you may actually find you are drawn to the internal side of the business and perhaps seek a position in human resources within that same company. You will have eliminated finance from your interest and replaced it with human resources. Or you may love the finance side of your job but cannot stand New York, so you take your next job at an investment-banking firm in Charlotte, North Carolina. Through these selections and eliminations, you move a little bit deeper into the Funnel.

> **Something I have learned:** The path inside the Funnel is not linear. You will zigzag around even while you hone in on what you most enjoy.

Early in your career, most people have big zigs and zags as our decisions either remove or select large chunks of industries or types of work. Over time, the path down the Funnel typically becomes straighter, or at least the zigzags become tighter. Your decisions are no longer "I don't like healthcare" but rather "I don't like implementation phases of IT within the hospital sector of the healthcare industry." If you are at this point of elimination, you have probably already decided you like the healthcare industry, you like the hospital sector of the healthcare industry, and you like the IT side of the hospital sector of the healthcare industry. Your zag about implementation has smaller implications for your overall career. This means you are moving closer to your Funnel Stem.

THE FUNNEL STEM

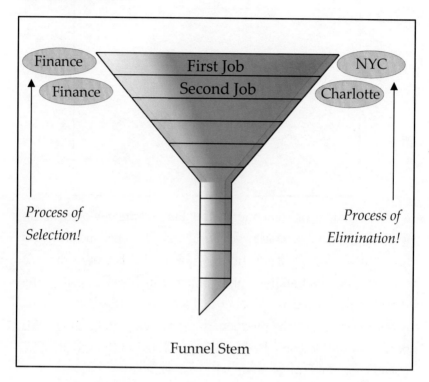

Funnel Stem

Through an ongoing series of selections and eliminations, you will move to different jobs, experiences, and potentially places. You will also move deeper into the Funnel of your career, getting you closer to your Funnel Stem, which is the ideal place to be professionally. The Funnel Stem is where three areas overlap:

1. You are well compensated.
2. You are good at your job.
3. You are passionate about the work you are doing.

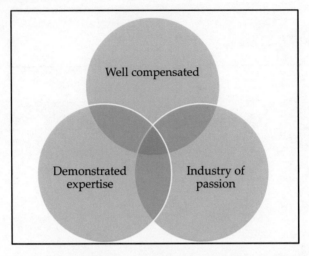

An example of someone in the Funnel Stem would be an individual who is good at negotiating and planning, and who also loves the outdoors and adventure, who then lands a job as the vice president of merchandising at a company such as Patagonia. She is well compensated as a VP, her skill set matches her role, and she is passionate about the products she is sourcing and selling. This person would probably be incredibly satisfied professionally. She would be in the Funnel Stem of her career.

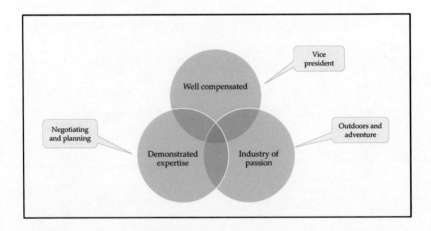

Liquid moves through a funnel slowly, as there is more volume at the top than can fit through the narrower stem at the bottom, creating friction. The Funnel Stem is where your career has no friction, and you are no longer making large-scale decisions of elimination and selection. The Funnel Stem is when work doesn't feel like work. It is where you say to yourself, "I can't believe I am getting paid to do this."

Imagine a world where everyone is doing work that they enjoy and are good at doing in an industry or field in which they have passion. The cumulative productivity of our nation would be insane. So how do you end up here? How do you maneuver yourself toward the intersection of these three areas? Where do you start? When I speak to different audiences and individuals about the Funnel and the Stem, my first advice is simply *do something*.

Do something? What the hell does that mean?

> **Something I have learned:** Do something, as something will lead to something else.

All of you are somewhere in the Funnel. Once you start in it, you cannot reverse out of it. By the simple passing of time and experience, you are all positioned to make choices of Selection and Elimination.

WORK YOU ARE GOOD AT DOING

Early in your career, first focus your discovery on the circle of "work you are good at doing." When I reference "work you are good at doing," think generally about these types of categories: sales, marketing, finance, IT, operations, human resources, and strategy. These sectors of work can apply to almost every company and industry.

> **Something I have learned:** *Early in your career, the first goal should be to try to hone in on the work you enjoy and excel at doing, with less focus on the specific industry or company.*

I was meeting with a person once who was trying to figure out the next phase of her career, and she was interested in consulting. She also potentially had a path in healthcare IT. She was very concerned about which path to take. What she didn't realize was that within both of these industries, there are jobs in sales, marketing, finance, IT, operations, human resources, and strategy. She was concerned more about the industry than the type of work she would be doing. The industry itself won't necessarily help you find the work you are good at doing, as similar types of jobs are available across industries.

When you take a job in one of these main sectors, you can reflect on whether you enjoy the functional activities of your job and whether you are good at the work. If, for instance, you are working for a technology company in a training type of job, then you are doing operations. You may realize you are not great at training other people because you don't have the attention to detail, but you realize you are terrific at making relationships with the people you are training. That may mean you would excel at and enjoy sales rather than operations. Begin the Funnel process by selecting and eliminating the type of work you excel at and enjoy doing, then turn your focus to the industries that most interest you.

> **Something I have learned:** *A critical point to Selection and Elimination, though, is that there is no singular, correct path!*

Soak in this statement, as it can be critically helpful, especially when you are at points of frustration in your career. There is no defined or "perfect" path for you through the Funnel, because most people are generalists. Even those who are born with some fairly unique skill are actually generalists. Why? Because we tend to be good at more than one thing. And because our skill sets are subtle and surface slowly over time. I admire people who love something. My daughter loves animals. She *loves* them. She loves animals with a depth of passion more than any of my passions. Even now, she tells me she wants to operate a pet orphanage. Whether she does this or not, as a nine-year-old she has something I don't have: a highly focused passion. She could pick from a handful of careers right now and already be deep in the Funnel. Not me, though. I am a generalist. I like a lot of things and I am decent at many things, but none of them strikes me as the professional "North Star." Many, if not most, of you are this way, too. You don't have a single right answer for the question of "What do you want to do?" because there isn't one. You could find success and fulfillment in many careers. As such, it takes you longer to find the Funnel Stem. The critical goal, then, is to accelerate the process of finding the Funnel Stem.

INTENSE PERSONAL REFLECTION

The only controllable way to get to the Funnel Stem more quickly is through Intense Personal Reflection (IPR). IPR means constantly asking yourself questions about what you like and dislike about your profession.

> **Something I have learned:** You should routinely take a step back and do some personal reflection on important professional questions.

13

What I mean by routinely is that on a monthly, weekly, and sometimes daily basis, you should consider some of the following questions:

> How are you spending your time at work?
> Do you like how you are spending your time at work?
> Have you enjoyed most of the projects assigned to you over the past month?
> Does your work seem to come naturally to you?
> Do you like the culture of the company you work for?
> Do you generally appreciate the people you work with?
> Are you putting forth the intensity that will allow you to be considered for the next interesting work that comes along?
> If you could only spend two hours this week on work, what would you spend that time doing?
> Are you working in an industry that generally interests you?

These are some of the core questions that help you move deeper into the Funnel. They are important to consider on a regular basis because they serve as the framework for the Process of Elimination and Selection. Although difficult, it is essential to be patient as well. You should not expect all of these answers to be yes all the time, but generally, over time, you should be moving in a direction toward products, services, and industries that are interesting to you. You should be moving toward work that you are good at doing and toward parts of the world or country in which you want to live. These are some of the core questions and reflections that help you move down through the Funnel. These are also the core questions that give you angst and can make you feel dissatisfied and discontented.

You might dig into some serious IPR, get some answers, and know where you want to go next and what you want to do, only to find that none of the doors open for you right away. This friction of timing will probably create anxiety and frustration. Try to acknowledge that this is the position you are in *for now*. Be confident and assured in the knowledge that you actually have done some Intense Personal Reflection and have found some answers. The reflection and the answers are accomplishments in themselves. Remember, there is no single, correct path. The vice president at Patagonia likely took a long and winding path to get there and probably had some diversions to places or jobs that were not perfect but at the time were pushing her in the correct direction.

It's also important to note that some uncertainty is okay. Our passions tend to evolve and change. Again, the key question is not "What do you want to do?" as in forever, but rather "What could I do now that feels right?" If you continue to reflect and follow what you could do now that feels right, your career will unfold for you and you will have a chance at getting to the Funnel Stem. Getting to the Funnel Stem, though, is not an entitlement. It is not something you deserve or are owed. Many people never get to that place where they are well compensated for a job they are good at doing in an industry that excites them. Some may only get one of these at the best point of their career. Some may get two, and the very lucky few may get all three. Part of the outcome is up to you, part of it is up to luck or timing, and part of it is up to other life circumstances for you. Your career is a big part of your life, but it is only part of your life. Take heart in knowing that you are being as proactive and thoughtful in the process of determining your career as possible.

I graduated from college in May and stumbled upon my first job in the healthcare industry. This was by no means my dream job, but I felt lucky to have a job immediately after graduation in the industry I loved. After spending a few months in this job, I quickly learned that the role would not fulfill my long-term goals. I did not know which industry or role would best position me to achieve my future goals, but I had a strong feeling I had to move to be successful. I had a choice—either stay in my current role and hope for the best, or venture into a completely new career.

I had tons of ideas, but I was extremely overwhelmed, anxious, and unsure of where to begin. I knew I loved healthcare, but also found myself interested in other industries. I knew I enjoyed working in team settings, but also enjoyed IT and tech. I found myself constantly going around in circles with an unclear direction of where I wanted to go. I would be happy doing a variety of things—but what would make me the most successful? One option would be to go into consulting (like every other recent grad at my university). It was a safe option, my parents would approve, and I would have mobility across many industries. I could go into IT and work with computers and medical software systems. I also toyed with the idea of going into operations, since I enjoy logistics and efficiency. Not to say I am a renaissance woman who can do it all, but there are a lot of paths that would take me in vastly different directions.

I met with as many people as I could to get their feedback. My parents, my parents' friends, career counselors at my university, and higher-ups at neighboring hospital systems . . . the list goes on. Everyone seemed to have a bias in one direction. I valued all of the advice I obtained, but none of it gave me the context to address my feelings and move forward. I needed help clearing my mind and focusing on my main objective.

Seeing the Funnel made so much sense! In the broadest part of the Funnel were the specific entry-level roles (sales, consulting, IT). Each ring of the Funnel would be a career step that brings me closer to my overarching goal. For instance, maybe at the broadest level I could go into sales. Sales might then bring me into consulting, and then I might realize I love consulting and eventually become a partner. Or I may find that I enjoy IT healthcare consulting, and so I end up moving to another firm, taking nonlinear steps upward until maybe I start my own company or end up in my dream job. The point being that my career would most likely not be a straight line, and I couldn't move forward with my end goal in mind because it was not realistic for me to know what my end goal was at the time. I had to focus on doing the next right thing for me now. Some of the most valuable advice that I now give to all my friends looking to change their careers or trying to find their first job is to always take the next best step. It is not about the future, but about the next step that presents the best opportunity in that moment.

I also understood the different roles someone could have in almost any company: sales, IT, supply chain, ops, finance, etc. I now get that the higher positions in a company eventually contain several of these areas. For instance, CEO contains all of them. VP of marketing could include sales and marketing. CFO could include finance and operations. This helped me understand that if I enter a company I like, I most likely can move laterally within that company over time. This flexibility would allow me to find the role that works best for me and follow the career path of my choosing.

I greatly appreciate the Venn diagram with the three circles labeled "Demonstrated Expertise," "Well Compensated," and "Industry of Passion." In the middle where they all meet is your dream job. I focused first on what my desired role was. Using the Venn diagram, I looked for a role where I would gain exposure to different areas and hone in on what I enjoy doing the most. Next, I would work on finding the industry. If I liked sales, I could do sales in any company in any industry. Lastly, I understand that generally the longer you work in jobs you enjoy and the more experience you have in an industry you enjoy, the higher your compensation will likely be. The ultimate goal for me is to end up in the middle to be happy and successful at the same time.

All of this gave me a sense of clarity. I felt organized and in control. I think the biggest struggle of the modern workforce is that we tend to be anxious that the choices we make now will determine the rest of our lives. We also want direct, linear progression where we see the fruits of our labor immediately. In reality, there are a lot of ways we can go about achieving our goals. Everyone has a different path, so there is no wrong decision. It all comes back to making the next best step.

This stuff stuck with me, and I ended up taking my next best step. I interviewed with companies that aligned with my Common Thread. Some companies I loved but did not get the job; others didn't connect with me, but I did receive an offer. Eventually, I applied to a job in sales with a healthcare consulting firm. I said to myself with relief going into the interviews, "If I get an offer, I know this is my next best step." I ended up receiving an offer and moving to a new and exciting city two weeks later. I love my job and my company, and one day I hope to achieve my long-term goals with this firm. In the meantime, I will continue to take the next best step in my career.

—Allie W., Client Management Associate

2
HOW AM I EVER GOING TO GET OR CHANGE JOBS?

This is one of the most common questions I get asked. More specifically, when I talk about my own career, people are surprised by the random jump I made from discount retailing into healthcare. They want to know how I made that specific transition, because so often people feel stuck. Again, most of you don't know the industry you want to work in when you begin your career. You just try to find a decent job, and then over time you migrate into an industry that suits you. You can feel trapped, though, when you discover that the job or industry you chose isn't what you want but you don't know how to get out of it. Feeling trapped in the wrong industry sucks. You crave that connection to purpose, and after you have explored an industry and then discover that it does not have the alignment that you desire, you again feel off track or off pace of your career.

These same feelings can apply to getting a job. When you are unemployed, finding work can be consuming. You live in a state of uncertainty and often face one closed door after another. It's enough to challenge the confidence of even the most confident people. What's more, the actual task of getting a job or switching jobs is painstaking. I would argue that the internet has actually made applying for jobs much more difficult than it used to be. It is one place that has created inefficiency. Prior to online applications, a person actually had to purchase a newspaper, read through the classifieds, type up a résumé, print it out, type a letter, put both documents in an envelope, buy a stamp, and put the envelope in a mailbox. These are all incredibly basic human tasks, yet the fact that you had to do this actually filtered out a bunch of lazy people, so there was generally less competition for jobs. With everything online now, the effort required to apply for a job is minimal. In fact, it is too easy. As such, companies have many more résumés to filter through, which significantly reduces the time the hiring manager spends considering each candidate. This entire process is like sitting in an airplane on the runway with a delayed flight and the pilot is not giving you any information on why the delay is occurring or when you might actually take off. It is a completely powerless feeling (and also maddening). You just want to know if you are qualified for the job or not. You want to know whether you should focus on this opportunity or move on to another one. You crave an actual human connection, which has become rare in the modern application process.

> **Something I have learned:** The rules of the application game now stink, so it is essential to change the game.

SEPARATE YOURSELF

The key to changing the game is to separate yourself from everyone else. The way you separate yourself from everyone else is:

1. Apply differently.
2. Be the most prepared.
3. Talk about them, not you.

The first way to separate yourself is to break the rules of application. If you see a position that interests you or if you find a company you want to work for, one tactic is to go straight to the top. Many times, when I was in a sales position, I sent a letter directly to the CEO of a company to explain our product or service. I didn't know the person at all and they had never heard of me. This same approach can be used to get a job. Go ahead and do the online application part. Your primary goal, however, is to go old school. You need to differentiate yourself, and there is a very simple way to do so. Go to the website of the company you want to work for and look for the link to the "About" or "Leadership" page. Typically, the names of the CEO, COO, and occasionally the vice president of human resources are listed. You are going to send a packet to as many of these three positions as you can find. You are going to blindly send a letter to the CEO of the company. Is that awkward and kind of weird? Yes. Who the hell cares, though? The CEO might throw it away or you just might capture enough of her attention to get her to walk down the hall and put it on the desk of the VP of human resources.

Your packet should include a cover letter and your résumé. Print these out on high-quality paper, but nothing cheesy. Stay away from color and texture. You are not entering a scrapbooking contest, you are trying to get a job. Your letter is much more important than your résumé. An essential part of your letter is that *the content of your letter should be more about their company than you*.

> **Something I have learned:** *They don't care about you. They want to know what you can do for them, so talk about them.*

I was working with a young professional recently who was interested in the advertising field. When we sat down to talk, she immediately began to talk about her experience and background and current work. These things are important, but they are important later in the interviewing process. Her—and *your*—first goal is to get noticed, and you actually don't get noticed by talking about you. You get noticed by talking about them. She was interested in one firm in particular, so I suggested that she find out through the company's website who their big clients were. I then suggested she study the work that the company did for those clients. She needed to submerge herself in the work of the advertising firm and know it extensively. If, for example, the company did advertising for a bank, then she should research and study all the digital and print media the firm had created for that bank. She also should actually get in the car and go visit one of the branches of the bank. Yes, it would be absolutely awkward to walk into a random bank and just look around. The key, though, is being able *to say* that you actually did that. You need to be able to tell the story of you going to a random bank later in the interview process. You need to get credit for being that diligent. All of this diligence will feed into your process of separating yourself.

For your cover letter, you now want to take all this research and extra effort and weave it into your letter. Again, they don't know you or care about who you are, so you want to separate yourself by talking about them. Your letter is a sneaky way to express how you are different and should look something like the following:

September 24, 2017

Ms. Jane Smith, CEO XYZ Marketing Company

123 Hire Me Street

Anytown, Ohio 33323

Dear Ms. Smith:

We have not met, but I want to work for your company. I have done the following activities, which I don't think any candidate has likely done before interviewing with your company:

Researched who your clients are on your website and picked the top one that intrigued me: First Bank.

Viewed every commercial and social media campaign that you did for First Bank since you began supporting them in 2015.

*Visited a First Bank branch here in town and talked to
their manager about the marketing campaign you did for
them to learn how it affected their business.*

*I appreciate the way that your company brought to life
the message of "Technology making life easier for First
Bank's customers." The message resonates on their
website, on their app, and inside the branch. The branch
manager actually noted a few customers that week who
commented on the new website.*

*It is difficult for young professionals to make a distinction
in today's online career-application process, so I am
sending this to you personally. I am very interested in
your open position of Creative Associate. My work ethic
is representative of the activities I noted above. If you
have a moment, I would sincerely appreciate you
dropping my letter and résumé on the desk of your human
resources manager.*

Best personal regards,

Frazer Buntin

I know this sounds like I am turning you into a stalker. Trust me: it's worth it. You will be amazed at how this can work. CEOs can relate to several aspects of this letter, and many will appreciate the confidence of someone junior having the guts and foresight to go directly to them. I have been a CEO twice in my career, and I will tell you that I would have advanced this type of letter through the hiring process *every time*. Many leaders will appreciate the initiative proven by someone actually going that far to research and understand their business. Many leaders will actually walk down the hall and give your packet to the head of human resources.

When you send the letter, don't fold it and send it in a normal envelope, as these end up in the trash. Go to a FedEx store and have it mailed priority mail, unfolded, in a letter-size envelope. People think FedEx mail is important and always open it. Mail that comes in a normal envelope is the equivalent of spam.

CREATE YOUR SKIT

Now that you have the attention of the human resources department, the next step is to absolutely nail the interview. To do this, you need to take your research and preparation to a whole new level. How? There's a specific methodology that works, and I have a story that helps illustrate it.

Early in my career, when I had been working at Dollar General for seven years, I realized I needed to make a change. I had enjoyed my time there and I appreciated the foundation of valuable business skills I had gained. But I was ready for something new (Process of Elimination). I knew I wanted to stay in Nashville, where I was living at the time (Process of Selection), and I knew I wanted to be in an industry that had a greater potential for more disruption and change (Process of Selection). I targeted healthcare because Nashville has many healthcare companies and it's an industry of ongoing innovation. I then zeroed in on a company called Healthways as the place where I wanted to work. Healthways was doing interesting work, they were disrupting the industry, and they were known for having a great company culture. I believed I could switch jobs and industries and set out to do so.

The most difficult part about switching industries is that you are competing for jobs against people who are already in that industry. For me, I was competing with a bunch of people who already had healthcare experience. A critical element to beating these folks is to be more prepared than everyone else who walks in the door for those jobs. In fact, that's the critical element for landing any job, whether it's your first or one much further down in the Funnel.

I started with a key milestone and worked backward. The key milestone, when getting or switching jobs, is to be able to sit in an interview and blow away the person you are talking to at the company. Not just to impress them, but rather to blow them away. They need to think you might be one of the best applicants they have ever met for any job. This was my goal. My first goal was not the job itself, but the opportunity to interview for the job. I felt if I could get in front of the right person and have enough preparation, I could bring it home. I would not just impress the person interviewing me, I would blow him away. That was my goal. To reach it, I decided I needed to create a "Skit" that would make me appear as if I were more capable of supporting their company's needs than anyone who had ever walked in the door to interview. I needed to bring the most A-game in the history of A-game. So I spent about four months working on my Skit. I busted my ass on this Skit. My Skit was the shit.

The Skit is composed of three sections:

1. What is going on in the larger industry? (In my case, healthcare.)

2. How does the company you are going after play into the overall industry dynamic?
3. How could my skills and experience align with what the company is doing within the overall industry?

To create my Skit, I needed content and a story. For the content, I looked at Healthways' website. If the company you have targeted is a publicly owned company, the best place to go for content for your Skit is the part of the website called "For Investors" or "About Us." These links are often found in the footer as opposed to the main navigation bar. Down there, you will also find links to a bunch of official-looking documents called things like 10-Ks. These are documents that public companies have to create as part of being a public company. Think of the documents as disclosures for existing and potential investors. The two best documents to find are:

1. The Annual Report, which is a document that every public company creates every year at the end of their fiscal year. Inside this report, you can read a letter from the CEO to the investors, identifying strengths of the business, risks to the business, evaluation of performance, projections on future performance, explanation of the status of the industry, and all kinds of other information. This content is gold for your Skit. Print this stuff out and take a highlighter to it. Yes, print it out and go old school on it.
2. Company Overview. Sometimes a public company will create and post a PowerPoint presentation on their website. Same deal: print this mother and go to work on it.

If the company is not public, look on the website anyway. Search the internet and read every article you can find on the company. You will slowly start to understand how the company works, who their customers are, and other relevant pieces of information, which you will use for content for the "middle" of your Skit. The middle part of your Skit will be when you wow the person you are meeting with by knowing more about their company than anyone who has ever sat across from them. You will know more because you will have taken the Annual Report, the articles, the Company Overview, and anything else you could get your hands on and you will have studied it, underlined things, looked stuff up, made notes, etc. until you have developed a thorough understanding of what the company does. Specifically, you should know who their customer is, what service they provide, how the industry is changing, how their service is changing, how their financial performance is, what business challenges they face, and what strategic changes they are making. These are essential.

If you have the ability to experience firsthand the service of the company, do it! When I interviewed applicants for positions with Dollar General, the first question I asked them was "When was the last time you were in a Dollar General store?" I was amazed at the number of people who applied for a job with the company who never thought that it might be a good idea actually to go see what the hell the company does! There were nine thousand freaking stores to choose from, and many of them didn't go to one of those before coming to the interview! Why should I hire them?

So again, if you can experience the company's service, do it. If you are applying for a real estate–development job, find a building that the company developed and go walk around it. If you are applying for a sales position, try to buy the product the company is selling. The more you can experience the service or product of the company you are targeting, the better your Skit will be. This experience is absolute gold for the middle part of your Skit.

Studying and experiencing the company is not enough. You need to write it all down. Imagine you actually get the interview with this company and the first question they ask you is "Tell me everything you know about our company, what we do as a business, and why our customers like us." Write down your answers using your notes and the material you found on the website, the experience you had with their service or product, the feedback other employees gave you, and anything else you can weave into the material. Then throw away the piece of paper and write it all down again.

Then do it again.

Then again.

Then again.

Do this at least once a day for a month. At the end of the month, you won't need to write it down as you will know it by memory. Did I mention the Skit is hard? It takes work and it takes time. You now have the middle part of the Skit complete. You also likely know something about the industry in which the company operates.

Now take this same methodology and hit the internet. Look for industry publications specifically that match with key industry words you found in the company-specific material. You will know these publications because they will be the most boring-looking publications you have ever seen. Again, print out articles and find the nuggets in them. Use the same question but broaden it to "Tell me everything you know about XYZ industry." Write down your answer.

Then again.

Again.

Again.

You now have part 1 and part 2 of your Skit complete.

FIND YOUR COMMON THREAD

The last part is to connect your specific skills and experience to the company and the industry. This is tricky but doable. You need a "Common Thread" from your career that you can connect to the company. Your Common Thread needs to have a lot of specific information from your life. If you have an interest in technology development and you are asked the question in an interview about what you are interested in, don't just say, "I am interested in finding a job in technology development." Of course you are. That's why you are in the interview, but that answer does nothing to separate you from other applicants. In order to shape a powerful answer, you need to give as much specific evidence to support your Common Thread as possible. When you are asked that question, imagine you are taking the person on a mental train ride of your life as it relates to technology development. If you are early in your career, your answer may sound like the following: "I have always had an interest in technology. It started in high school when I joined the Robotics Club. I was fascinated how. . . . I actually chose the college I wanted to attend because of their technology major. The lab work was incredibly valuable there for. . . . Finally, working on the SpaceX project as an intern sealed it for me, as I was able to see how all the different parts of a large-scale technology project come together. I now feel I have the foundation to apply my past experience to a position that . . ." This answer tells a story. Yes, the story is about your life, but instead of a plain old chronology, the framework is your Common Thread, which allows you to then tie your own experiences directly into the company interviewing you. Some Common Threads are more obvious than others, so if you have not had a consistent passion in your career, you may have to dig deeper to see yours. It's also possible that you may have more than one Common Thread.

I used "decentralized operations" as my Common Thread, which may seem fairly obscure, but it was true. What I meant by "decentralized operations" was that my logistics experience, my buyer experience, and my store-operations experience at Dollar General were all in an environment or business setting of decentralized operations. We had nine thousand very small stores all over the United States. It is impossible physically to be at all of these stores all of the time, so we had developed business processes that enabled decentralized operations. I could name dozens of examples of initiatives I had led, lessons learned, vendors worked with, tools and tactics implemented—all to support a company characterized by decentralized operations. This was my story. This is what made me a special snowflake. To the hiring manager, I was all of a sudden an expert at decentralized operations, never mind that I had no specific healthcare experience.

I then wove this Common Thread into Healthways' business. I thought about all their areas of decentralized operations, including ten different call centers, remote employees, and a variety of acquired businesses with decentralized operations. They had evolved from a single site in Nashville to a semi-decentralized business. Additionally, I discovered one of the businesses they had acquired had a very strong decentralized nature. Bingo! Holy crap, what a find! I had my last critical part of the Skit. In preparing for the interview, I then pretended to answer the question of "Tell me about what you have been doing."

> **Something I have learned:** Hiring managers always ask some variation of the question "Tell me about what you've been doing." Do not answer with a boring chronology of your work life.

Rather than going from job to job to job in my explanation as most people do, I framed my response on the Common Thread of decentralized operations. Almost every day for three or four months at Dollar General during lunchtime, I went into a conference room, closed the door, and wrote out the Skit on a whiteboard and practiced it over and over verbally. For four months I did this same routine.

HIJACK THE INTERVIEW

Once I was able to get an interview with the company, I used another incredibly valuable tactic. I call it hijacking the interview. Most hiring managers are terrible at interviews because it is something they do not do very often. When we don't do something often, we don't develop skills and competencies at that activity. The questions in interviews are usually predictable and end up being more conversational about work experience and the needs of the company. As such, interviews are very easy to hijack. First, why would you want to hijack an interview? Well, you just spent four months busting your ass to research and create a damn Skit, and they aren't simply going to ask you to recite it, so you need to answer a question that *they won't actually ask you*! Additionally, if they ask you a question that you can't answer well, you need a canned answer that you can apply to their question. Most of your canned answer will be some or all of your Skit. For example, if you are indeed asked the typical question of "Tell me what you have been doing or what you are doing now," you were just given the easiest lay-up, and hijacking the interview is cake. They had no intention of you going off on an explanation of their industry or their company, but that is fine.

When I got this question at Healthways, my answer probably actually started out with me saying something such as the following: "I have spent the past seven years mastering how to lead operations that are decentralized in nature. I focused on this area because I have been amazed at the number of companies now that are decentralized in nature. Take Healthways for example . . ." I was then off to the races with the Skit. I simply hijacked the interview and probably spent the next five to eight minutes talking nonstop about their industry, their company, and how my Common Thread would benefit them. I didn't let the interviewer interrupt me once, as I needed to get it all out. Once the Skit has opened the door for the conversation, you will find that the interviewer will actually begin to talk more and explain more about their company and their industry. The Skit changes the entire dynamic of the interview. When the interview was over, I practically floated out of the room, as I knew I had nailed it. It was a great feeling.

Getting a better job or moving to an industry that suits you better is difficult. I probably spent collectively over one hundred hours simply preparing for one interview. You are going to have to put in the work to make it happen, but if you put in the work, your likelihood of success will increase significantly. It is important to note, though, that each of these steps builds on the other, and all are required to improve your odds. You won't know which of the steps may be the critical piece, so incorporating all of them into your plan is essential.

Throughout the process, you will wonder if all of this work is worth it. You will wonder if the hours you are investing in researching a company or an industry or creating a Skit that you may never get to use are worth it. Acknowledge that those feelings are normal and trust that your research and Skit writing and practice will be applied to something further down the Funnel than where you are today.

Lastly, remember how badly you wanted to get that first or next job. Remember those feelings when someone else reaches out to you who is looking for their next job and asks if you will talk to them. Try to take the calls and give those people who are searching fifteen minutes of your perspective or your guidance. Explain the path of your career. Acknowledge their feelings and give them some direction on what helped you. It is challenging to find time to talk to all of the people who may want to network with you, but there is some humanity in paying it forward by pulling the next person up the wall behind you.

The anxiety of setting yourself apart as a candidate, of proving to a perfect stranger that you are unique, capable, and a risk worth taking, is an all-consuming, fear-inducing place to be. You know you have special qualities to offer and drive to boot. Proving this on paper, where your personality can be lost and your accomplishments look run-of-the-mill, is an entirely overwhelming task. The methods in this chapter break apart the process into various phases and employ tactical skills such as research, flattery, breaking apart interview questions into themes, and old-school handwriting to set yourself apart from other candidates.

Having chosen my desired career, I applied to ten agencies in the hopes of working in a collaborative environment, rather than independently as I had been for two years. As the weeks stretched on and I awaited feedback, a few emails trickled in, all beginning with the cut-and-dry "Dear Candidate, thank you for your application but . . ." The majority of the agencies did not respond to my emails. I was not special; I did not have enough to offer. These insurmountable feelings of inferiority and failure consumed me. But again and again, those around me would reiterate that I had so much to offer and that I had natural talent and promise.

I kept pushing. I knew something about my approach had to be falling short. So I changed my tactics. Instead of working toward a stronger presentation of myself, I instead started researching the companies to which I was applying. I started at the top of my list and spent serious time looking up articles about the company, what they were doing in the industry, their mission statement, and how it related to my own pursuits; I researched their company history, how they grew, each employee's LinkedIn; I chose three client profiles of theirs that I found interesting and pulled examples as I composed my portfolio letter. This became my "old-school" method of separating me from everyone else. Everything I learned about this company became an opportunity to relate back to myself, my strengths, and my interests. In this way, I was framing myself as familiar territory for the company.

After mailing a hard copy of my portfolio, along with a handwritten note, I got a call for an interview. I'd been here before and had fallen short on setting myself apart. This time, I went into overdrive. I continued my in-depth research of their client work by visiting the locations and taking note of my experience and what I appreciated about the work. I compiled a list of potential interview questions and prepared a slew of broad answers that could fit multiple questions. These "themes" helped develop a stream-of-consciousness approach to anything I could be asked. I was prepared to answer with information-packed responses that could open the conversation up on a personal level. This was my Skit. It was well-researched, detailed, rehearsed, and heartfelt.

Before the interview, I reminded myself of two important steps: chill the hell out, and embrace life's question mark. Regardless of the outcome, I was certain I had done my best. The week after my interview, I sent a second handwritten letter thanking my interviewers for their time. Two days later, I received an email. This *time, it was a personalized message welcoming me to the team. My hard work had paid off and I had finally launched my career! Without these methods, I do not believe I would have been able to set myself apart and conclude my interview with such confidence. My personal attributes were present all along, but these tactics taught me how to present them in a way that is effective across all disciplines and in any type of interview situation.*

—Andie E., Graphic Designer

3
I FEEL LIKE NO ONE CARES ABOUT MY CAREER

Many of you have had professors, coaches, guidance counselors, or parents who have led you along in life. You then enter your career and now no one is there who is really helping. This feels strange and different. You want someone to guide you, promote you, and give you constant feedback, coaching, and professional development. You may feel that your manager should pick up your career, throw it on her back, and charge the mountain of life with you. In reality, it doesn't happen this way. Most of your career decisions will be made by you.

You will be the primary driver of the unfolding of your career. As such, you may feel as if you are alone in determining the progression of your career. You may feel alone in deciding which job to do next or how to get it. You may feel alone in determining if you are on track with what you should be doing.

ANNUAL REVIEW

Instead, the career support that most managers provide is through the annual review. Let's dig into the annual employee-review process. The annual review is often painful for everyone. It is painful for the manager because most managers don't do routine (monthly) performance check-ins with their employees to share candid feedback. Managers don't usually do this because it is uncomfortable to tell people the things they are not doing well. The end-of-the-year performance review comes along, and often the feedback is completely generic or employees are surprised to discover they are not all-star performers. If managers have not been keeping notes and documentation of actual examples of exceeding expectations or not meeting expectations, the end-of-the-year review is generally useless. The feedback from the manager is vague and rarely ties to anything specific for the actual employee. The employee receives the review and is either glad there was nothing uncomfortable talked about or disappointed that there was not more tangible feedback.

I actually have never seen a performance-feedback model that has really struck me as exceptional. I haven't seen any company nail this stuff. The goal of an annual review is to measure performance against a set of tangible goals ideally based on monthly reviews that give real-time feedback. Most managers don't do these interim feedback sessions, though, because to do an effective monthly review, they need to capture examples of exceptional or substandard performance as it occurs. To capture these examples, they actually need to save an email from an employee, type up notes from a conversation or occurrence with the employee, or have some way of documenting how the employee either did a good job or bad job with a specific task. These small tasks provide the information and framework for an effective monthly review, which in turn provide the information and framework for an effective annual review.

I have seen very few managers use these methods. Most managers get to the end of the year, give most employees a middle-of-the-road rating, and hope none of their employees challenge the rating. Everyone is glad when they are over. This process is about the best that most employees get for professional development or support from their manager.

GOOD MENTORS ARE UNICORNS

There are some unicorns out there, though: managers who enjoy and excel at helping their employees improve at their job and develop in their career. I have had a few of these in my career. When you luck into one of these managers, use them for all they are willing to offer. If you don't have one of these managers, though, you need to look elsewhere for guidance.

Your best bet for finding someone who cares about your career is to seek out a mentor.

> **Something I have learned:** There are people within companies who enjoy listening and sharing feedback and suggestions to others about their career, but you have to know how to spot them.

There is a methodology for how you can find those people. Look for the people in meetings who don't necessarily talk the most or the loudest but usually make the most relevant or poignant points. Look for people who are observant of the business. Look for people who actually seem to care about the company you both work for. Lastly, look for people who are successful and are respected within your company. You want a mentor who knows what the hell they are doing.

The way to approach someone as a potential mentor is to start with a detailed question. It is very important that you have a detailed question. If you approach someone smart and successful and ask them a giant nebulous question, such as "What should I do to advance my career?" or "How can I get into a leadership position?" the prospective mentor will see you as naïve and a bunch of work. Those types of questions have hours and hours of answers, and these people don't have hours and hours of time to give to you. Start with something small. For example, if you are in a meeting with a potential mentor, try to get them for a few seconds at the end of the meeting or walking down the hall and give them the short version of your detailed question.

> "Hey, John. Can I get two seconds from you? I am really curious as to how purchasing works in our company and would love to get a fifteen-minute version of an explanation from you sometime. Let me know if you think I could find us a few minutes sometime in the next few weeks."

The types of people whom you want to be your mentor will potentially see a couple of things in your method and your question. First, they will respect that you have the guts to come talk to them. Second, they will appreciate the fact that you asked for only two seconds in the hallway. Third, they will appreciate that you are not actually asking them the question in the hallway expecting an answer then. Fourth, they will appreciate that you know to give their request a fifteen-minute window and not rush the request beyond a few weeks. If they are the type of person you want to have as a mentor, they will be willing to help educate another employee and explain how things work and will give you more than fifteen minutes.

When you meet with them, your goal is actually not to learn about whatever initial question you asked. You definitely want to ask the question, but more than anything, you want to start to connect with the person. You can connect with people using a couple of specific tactics. One tactic is to schedule the meeting on a Friday. Why? Think about what question everyone always asks on a Friday: "Do you have any big plans for this weekend?" Do NOT answer this question as "Not really." Why? Because that answer is boring as shit and no one wants to be around boring people! So if you can pull off a Friday meeting, you need to have something badass planned for the weekend like hang gliding or a triathlon or going to a music show. No kids' soccer games or yard work either. Yes, we all do it (or you will do it), but that's boring as shit too, so come up with something cool. Also, you actually need to do the activity that you mention because you want the mentor to see you the following week and ask you how your epic weekend activity was. You can't say you bailed out either. The other key reason for a Friday meeting is people are happier on Fridays and will be more likely to open up and perhaps talk longer than scheduled.

Another tactic for connecting with people is to observe their office when you come to meet with them. People's offices are generally a reflection of their interests. I always use this tactic in sales as well and have connected with people through all kinds of crazy things I have observed, including ceramic dolphins (no kidding), maps of the Caribbean, photography, and always pictures of kids. If you are good at very quickly connecting your experiences to whatever you see in the office, you can ask a personal question and they will usually open up and be more than willing to tell you that they have a map of the Caribbean on the wall because they love scuba diving. You can then tell them about your honeymoon to Turks and Caicos or a sailing trip to the Bahamas or a funny scuba-lesson story from college or whatever. It doesn't matter, as long as you let *them* talk about it and then briefly connect it to something from your life. You will often find the first twenty minutes of the conversation veer off on one of these types of topics. As a side comment, it can be a fun mental exercise to try to connect one of your own experiences to something anytime you enter someone else's office. See if you can find a connection within ten seconds.

So now you have found the time to meet with the prospective mentor and you want to give them some context around your question (i.e. interested in moving to a new department, observed something that sparked the question, etc.). Once you have provided the context, let them talk. When your time is up, simply thank them and leave. Don't ask for anything else. Don't suggest you get back together. Just thank them and leave. More than likely, the next time you see the person, they will ask you about the epic weekend activity you mentioned previously. Take a few minutes in the hall or breakroom or wherever and give them a concise but exciting recap of the weekend. Again, leave it at that. Several weeks later, think of another detailed work question and casually happen to run into the person and mention, "Hey, I have another random question for you if you ever have a few more minutes." There is a good chance the person will tell you to schedule time to come by their office to catch up. From there, find the right blend of personal and professional conversations to cultivate with this person. Congratulations—you now have a mentor. Your next objective is not to screw this up! The best way to screw up a mentorship is to overuse it. Requesting time with your mentor should be monthly at the most. Over time, you will end up spending less time with the mentor, but you may keep a relationship with that person over a long period of time. I have individuals whom I mentored years ago who still reach out to me a couple of times a year just to check in and occasionally ask for professional advice. I still enjoy my interactions with these people.

NETWORKS ARE CRITICAL

In addition to finding mentors, it is smart to build a professional network. These are people who are not quite friends but whom you purposefully keep in touch with on an ongoing basis. A professional network can include people you have worked with in the past, former bosses, others in your industry, or even people in other industries. You can use your network to help you solve problems, find people to hire, find a new job, and stay informed of industry news. You will have a few people in your network who can last a long time, and others who will come and go based on the work you are doing. I have a network of all kinds of people, including young professionals I have mentored to retired former CEOs. I keep up with one guy who owns a super high-end, Italian shoe company because I am interested in his industry, and he keeps up with me, perhaps because I can give him an outsider's view. I keep up with former investors to stay tuned into the new types of healthcare companies that are being created. I keep up with other leaders in the healthcare industry so I can stay informed of any new trends or developments in my industry. The way we stay connected may be through email or a call, or we may get together for lunch or coffee. I actually secured my first job at Evolent Health through my professional network. Find those people who are key influencers and industry leaders, and stay in touch with them periodically.

Again, don't come into your professional career expecting others to actively counsel you and guide you to your next role. This is *your* career, not your manager's. It is up to you to analyze your situation, explore options, and make the decisions about your future. You absolutely can and should seek input from others, including your manager. It is just important to consider that most of your managers may not be as active or skilled in this area as you expect. This will make you feel lonely and frustrated at first, but once you realize that you own the path of your career, it will be surprisingly liberating. The Funnel is yours, and you get to decide what goes in and what goes out.

> *As a college student, part of me definitely operated in the state that I can imagine many other college students around the world operate in: confusion. Confusion about what, how, when I should do, could do, would do. Definite confusion about why, too! For people in their early twenties who are transitioning from college life to real life, this confusion is often accompanied with a sense of anxiety and uncertainty and often fear, and this was the case for me too.*
>
> *Fortunately, I learned early on to reach out for help and input— and so I turned to professors, family members, and friends who had gone through the same journey. I heard much of the same—do what is right for me and trust in my instincts that have led me so far. My first real mentor—who still mentors me to date—came into my life right around this time. I think it was definitely encouraging to have someone who was able to understand my journey, having walked it*

at some point himself, but who was also able to understand how to provide guidance, how to coach, and who was able to stand solidly "in my corner" and say, "I believe in her."

Fast-forward a few months: I'm graduating, and applying for jobs—still testing out the waters, not 100 percent sure of what I should be doing. My mentor was able to provide guidance on some of the opportunities I was looking at and the kinds of questions I should be asking, as well as reaching out to some of his own networks to alert me to opportunities I should be considering.

When I decided to move back to Kenya, I again tested this decision with him. When I had a desk job that didn't suit me very well, he was able to listen and help me articulate exactly why I felt so uncomfortable and the kinds of lessons I should learn from the experience. Most recently, when I was exploring the idea of potentially joining a consulting firm, my mentor could push me, help me understand the value of this experience, and assuage my fears about whether I would be able to make it. About two years later, here I am as a consultant at McKinsey—still very actively working with my mentor! Now the conversation is about how to improve, what opportunities to take, and what feedback to act on.

For a mentorship to work, the relationship has to be organic, and it is not something that can be forced or assigned. Yes, I was assigned my mentor at an event—but the choice to take this relationship forward was something that happened organically. Additionally, you cannot expect your mentor to be operate the way a parent would—they are not psychic, and you have to make an effort to cultivate the relationship, reach out, ask questions, and communicate. My mentor is a few thousand miles away, but I make an active effort to keep him updated and to communicate—and sometimes, this may just be a quick hello. I'm definitely fortunate enough to have understood what people mean when they say that having mentors and sponsors are essential for your career, and lucky enough to have a mentor who has taught me (and continues to teach me) a lot. I've also learned to be mindful about making sure I pay it forward.

—Roshni W., Consultant

4
I Feel Like a Monkey Could Do My Job

Yes, there are times in your career when you will feel like a monkey could do your job. Actually, a monkey that got tequila-drunk last night, skipped dinner, woke up, and hasn't yet brushed its teeth but could still do your job. Some of you right now might be saying, "Holy shit! That is exactly how I feel!" For those of you who have never felt this way, just sit tight, as eventually you will. It absolutely sucks to feel this way. These are the times in your career when you wonder what you are doing, why you ever entered the field you did, how long you will be stuck in your job, and how you will ever get another one. Rather than jumping to what you should do to solve the problem, let's first deconstruct why you feel this way.

To deconstruct why you feel like this, I am going to throw some really bad PowerPoint skills at you. By modern corporate standards, I absolutely suck at making PowerPoints, but my PowerPoints are extremely clear in their message. I can't stand the amount of BS that goes into today's business PowerPoint presentations. I am a firm believer in bullet points and words instead of clip-art images and legends to explain those clip-art images. If you don't know what I am talking about, then just wait until you get a little higher in your company, and inevitably someone in your company will have worked for one of the big consulting firms where annual bonuses are based on the amount of clip art and arrows in their PowerPoints. I truly feel that if you gave a baby (yes, a baby) two different PowerPoint slides, each made out of plastic—one with blocks of bullet points and one with tons of images and arrows—and asked the baby (because babies can understand PowerPoint) to place the items on a piece of paper in a way that made sense, the babies would place the blocks of bullet points much faster. You get the point.

THE DEGREE OF STRETCH

First, think about how much a job challenges you. More specifically, how hard is your job to do? How difficult are the decisions you have to make? How complex is the work? How strenuous is the pace? How challenging are the problems you are trying to solve in your role? Let's call this perspective the Degree of Stretch, as it is a measure of how much the job you are in is "stretching you" professionally. For the chart below, assume the vertical axis of Degree of Stretch is an arbitrary measure of zero through three. Zero would be no stretch at all and three would be at the upper level of your capability professionally. Total stretch.

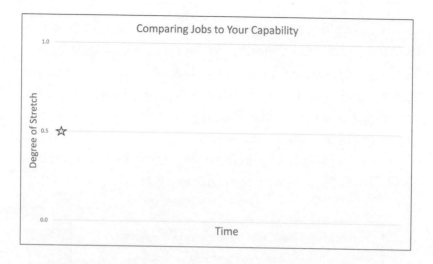

The horizontal axis shows time throughout your career. The yellow star represents your first job out of college. For most people, this will be somewhere in your early twenties. Let's arbitrarily give this job a 1.5 rating in Degree of Stretch. It is not totally easy because the field is likely new to you, but it is not overly difficult because it is an entry-level job. Let's also plot the star on the horizontal axis at the beginning (for obvious reasons).

Now let's plot the Degree of Stretch of this job over time.

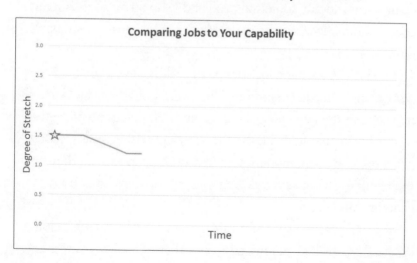

You can see that the Degree of Stretch cruises along at the same level for a while and then decreases for a period of time before flattening out again. Why does the Degree of Stretch begin to decrease and continue to decrease over time? Well, many jobs actually get easier over time. Why does the job get easier? It gets easier because you learn the requirements of the job, and with an entry-level job, you usually do those same activities in a repetitive nature. Basically, you do the same shit every day.

> *Something I have learned:* Entry-level jobs are generally hard as shit to get and easy as shit to do.

My first real job title was logistics planner for Dollar General Corporation. I chose this job through a somewhat ridiculous process. My brilliant twenty-two-year-old logic was to read the business section of the newspaper to see which companies were in the news. My thought was if a company is in the news, it was either doing something really good and I should look for jobs there, or the company was doing something bad and I should avoid it. Average companies rarely make the news. I know, this logic is questionable, but it worked.

I had no idea what a logistics planner did or even what logistics was or why it needed planning. Whatever, though. Dollar General had been in the news for building a nice new corporate office that was going to be state of the art with an onsite fitness center, cafeteria, and open, modern workspaces. It sounded like they had their stuff together. So I followed some of the steps I mentioned in chapter 2 and got the job.

My job was to use a software system to take merchandising orders that we had purchased from other companies across the country and bundle them into as close to full truckloads as possible. The software presented the location, weight, and cubic size of the order, and our goal was to use the fewest trucks as possible to move the merchandise. The fewer trucks required, the less total cost to move the merchandise and the more profit for our company.

At first this job was really tricky because the company had no training manual for us. I remember the first day sitting next to a woman who had been doing this job for years, watching her computer mouse move rapidly all over the screen as she right-clicked and added loads together, opened and closed screens, and did all kinds of crazy stuff. Several weeks later I decided I was ready to do all that crap by myself and moved into the seat with her next to me. I put my hand on the computer mouse and then did absolutely nothing. I was frozen. I had no idea really where to begin. One day, though, it clicked and I got it. After a few more weeks, I could do it in my sleep. I would add one-third of a truckload of mops to two-thirds of a truckload of Christmas wreaths, and SHAZAAM, a full truckload was created! Next it was fourteen thousand pounds and 680 cube of toilet paper combined with twenty thousand pounds and 1,300 cube of women's underwear coming from Bowling Green, Kentucky, to Fulton, Missouri, and then on to Ardmore, Oklahoma. I was a wizard. It was like using the video game *Tetris* (I'm old) for discount retailing. I used this same software system, routing truckloads of randomness for a year, essentially doing the same thing every day. Over time, though, the job became extremely routine and was no longer challenging for me. The excitement or even interest in my work declined in direct proportion to the decline in my Degree of Stretch.

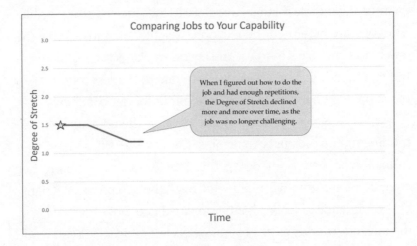

Ultimately, I reached the "monkey could do my job" point. Now, I don't mean to degrade entry-level jobs or to say that I actually feel that they are beneath me or anyone. Entry-level jobs are the foundation on which good business decision-making and leadership are built. The way you *feel*, though, is important to acknowledge, hence the monkey-business comments. That's how you feel.

THE LINE OF BOREDOM

Here is where this gets interesting. Once the Degree of Stretch of a job declines enough over time, eventually the job reaches the dreaded "Line of Boredom."

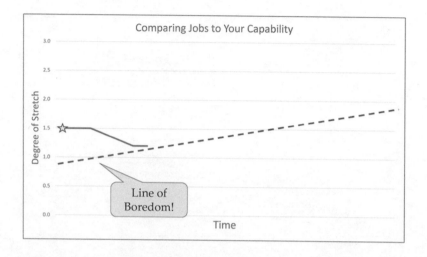

There is a point of boredom with almost any job. The Line of Boredom (LOB) represents the point at which you know your job so well that it is no longer interesting. You have figured it out and it really no longer challenges you. Your skills, knowledge, and capabilities are well beyond the work that you do on a routine basis. You are bored. You have the monkey tequila feelings. This is bad. This is also completely normal. Note that the LOB actually slopes upward over time. This means the further along you are in your career, the higher the Line of Boredom is because you typically take on harder jobs as your career unfolds.

So you are cruising along and you are doing your job well, but you are approaching your LOB. Then one day, BAM, your boss gives you a promotion or you take another job in another department or you take another job with a different company. The second yellow star represents the starting of that new job. For most people, each subsequent job is more challenging than the last one (or at least it should be). If it is not, then you will be moving from one LOB to another LOB. Don't do this. It sucks.

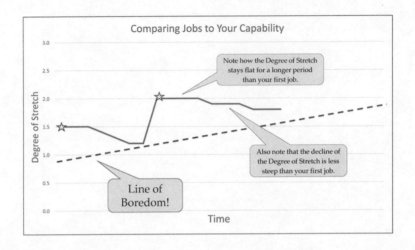

As your new job is likely more challenging than your last one, its Degree of Stretch starts on day one higher than any point of your previous job. Suddenly you are responsible for doing things with your new job that are new to you. Perhaps you now have to manage and lead a team of people. Or you may have moved into a new department and your entire job is different. Or you may have moved to a different company that has different processes for a similar job. Your job will feel stimulating again and your feelings of boredom will disappear. New challenges and experiences will fill you up and put you back in a place of fulfilled engagement.

Also note that in this new job you stay at that same initial Degree of Stretch for a longer period of time than you did in your first job. This is because higher-level jobs are harder to master. The duration of a high Degree of Stretch will typically lengthen for any new job as your career advances. This extended initial high Degree of Stretch means that, as you advance your career, each new job gets more challenging than the last because it takes longer to "figure out" the job. The result is that you stay interested in the job longer because it is more challenging. This helps you maintain a safe distance from the Line of Boredom.

For a while, at least. And then the same thing happens. The Degree of Stretch begins to decline for the same reason: you start to figure out how to do the new job, and over time it becomes easier. Depending on how long you stay around the Line of Boredom, you may begin to have the same feelings of being off track. And then it happens again. BAM. You get another job and the cycle continues.

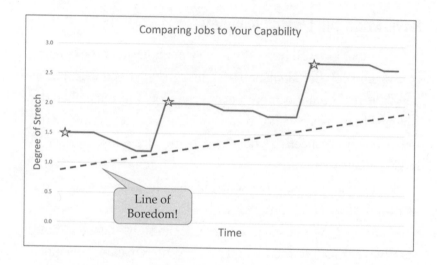

Note, however, the difference over time with the jobs. The Degrees of Stretch are longer and the declines shallower. The further along you are in your career, typically the longer it takes you to reach the Line of Boredom. I acted as interim-CEO of a company called White Glove Health for about six months when White Glove bought part of a company I had previously founded. When I joined the company, it was having strategic problems, financial problems, customer-retention problems, and employee-morale problems. I probably could have been in that role for years without ever coming close to the Line of Boredom. It challenged me and kept me engaged in many different areas. And yet, I stayed in it for only six months because the job required that I travel to

Austin, Texas, every week for six months to help stabilize the business. Even though the work was highly engaging, I did not want to move to Austin, so I covered as much ground as I could, hired a full-time CEO, and passed the reins over to him. By the Process of Elimination and Selection, I chose to eliminate Austin as a place I wanted to live and selected another path in the same healthcare industry.

NAVIGATING THE LINE OF BOREDOM

The more jobs you have, the more you understand the concept of the Line of Boredom and the more skilled you become at handling the situation more effectively. You will remember the feelings from before and you can then see them from that independent perspective and make better decisions on how to modify your situation.

We tend to use our professional life as a measuring stick of our identities. If we aren't on track within our professional lives, then who are we? We aggravate these feelings by benchmarking ourselves against our friends and peers. Who is making how much money? Who has what title? Many of these feelings come from a fear of being off-pace with life and from a desire to gain control over that pace. The fear of wasting time in your career is a strong one.

> *Something I have learned:* When you get to the Line
> of Boredom or start having monkey feelings, an intense
> restlessness arises.

Doubts flood your brain. Is this boring job setting me back a year of me becoming myself? What if I shouldn't even be in healthcare? Do I really like healthcare? You may feel like you are wasting time in your career, which then cascades into fears that you aren't even in the right industry. The next thing you know, you wonder why you are living in your apartment or city. Fight-or-flight kicks in. You want to hightail it out of there. This desire to flee is your attempt to control the situation. Again, you want to control the process of the unfolding of your career. When you arrive at this Line of Boredom and these feelings begin to creep into your mind, it is important to have awareness of what is going on with your job and your emotional reactions to your job. You need to see the situation from an independent angle or lens. Separate your emotions from your assessment of the situation. This awareness will prevent you from making a bad short-term decision. Sometimes you may need to leave the job, but leaving a job and fleeing a job are different actions.

Let's look at what can happen if you stay in a role at the Line of Boredom for too long. There are three possible consequences of hovering around the LOB for too long:

1. The quality of your work declines and you get fired.
2. You get another job within your company.
3. You quit and take a new job with a different company.

Number one is bad, so if you feel you are hovering around the Line of Boredom for too long, you need to do something about it, such as number two or number three. How? How do you change the situation? Remember and use the tactics in chapter 2 about getting or changing jobs—but wait! It is essential to understand how long you should allow yourself to stay in a job that is at the Line of Boredom. How long is too long?

> **Something I have learned:** *An absolute minimum for any job early in your career should be one year, and even that is short.*

If you are learning and absorbing everything you possibly can within your work environment even outside of your individual job, you won't likely reach the LOB faster than a year. I don't recommend staying at the same company your entire career, but I also strongly encourage completing multiple different roles at the same company. When you have several different jobs at the same company, your professional learning is accelerated as compared to doing those same roles in different companies. The reason for this acceleration is that within the same company, you will see how different pieces of the business connect. Having knowledge of these connection points is incredibly valuable to succeeding at a more senior level. Great CEOs are exceptional at seeing very quickly the connection points across different departments within their company, different companies within their portfolio of companies, and different companies within the industry overall. This skill is learned by seeing the dots connect over a career.

For example, at Dollar General I moved from the logistics department, where I was responsible for moving products, to the merchandising department, where I was responsible for purchasing the products. I was a much better buyer of our products because I understood the implications of my decisions on the shipping/moving side of the business. Later on when I was in the operations department, I could triangulate across all three functions extremely well. There were only a small number of people in the entire company of thirty thousand employees who had that perspective. In turn, that perspective made me more valuable as an employee because I performed better than my peers. I also was asked to participate in more of the interesting special projects because of my cross-departmental knowledge. When you participate in these special projects, you end up interacting with more senior people, which allows you to develop a professional network, explore even more new jobs, and become more known within the company. Additionally, that cross-departmental perspective made me more valuable as a potential hire for other retail companies.

So how long is too long to hang around the LOB? You need to be there long enough to engage in that Intense Personal Reflection we talked about in chapter 1. Note: this is difficult and you probably won't like it. Living around the LOB requires pant-loads of patience.

> **Something I have learned:** *A helpful way to remain patient while feeling bored and restless is to believe that even though you are bored and restless, you are on a good path.*

You can hang on, so long as you feel confident in the fact that you are conducting the Process of Selection and Elimination, you understand that you are at the LOB, and you have the playbook for how to navigate the next step in your career. Several different times while I was hovering restlessly at the LOB, a new component of my job would pop up and I would get pulled out of the LOB.

Eventually, you may get to jobs where you actually never reach the Line of Boredom. In these roles, you are constantly challenged and stretched and you actually never totally "figure out" the job. This is the sweet spot of your career. When you hit this point, your daily, weekly, and monthly activities are stimulating. Your work is interesting and meaningful over long periods of time, if not forever.

Early in your career, it is difficult to fathom this point actually exists, but it does.

You should expect to hit the Line of Boredom early in your career, though. You should expect to see the monkey. Don't hate him. Smile at him. Tell him you have him figured out and you know why he is there. Tell him he can hang out with you for a little while, but then he'll have to hit the road. Where you're going, he's not invited.

I graduated from university with an advertising degree during an economic crisis in 2008. Finding an entry-level job that I was remotely excited about, much less one in my field, felt virtually impossible. I'd just spent the past seventeen years investing in my education, why? So that I could be a waitress at a sports bar for the first five months post-graduation?

Eventually, I finally managed to find a temporary job in the corporate world (although, it was still less glamorous than I'd hoped). Rather than writing copy for brands or strategizing media buys like I'd practiced in my campaigns classes, I was scanning medical records into a database for eight hours a day. Over and over. I took the role because the company shared office space with the largest advertising agency in the state, and I hoped it would present opportunities for me to network. It didn't take long to learn the ropes (scan, click, save . . . seems pretty self-explanatory, right?). So in no time, really, I was feeling restless in my cave of an office with no windows. I tried to make the most of my circumstances: playing music I loved and telling myself, "At least you're not carrying chicken wings to strangers all day!" but it still felt incredibly frustrating to know I was capable of more than I was doing. I felt like a monkey could do my job. I continued to look for a permanent position in my field, telling myself surely this job crisis couldn't drag on forever. I interviewed for roles in New York, Chicago, LA—any city I was remotely interested in. Yet week after week, nothing was clicking into place and the monotonous sound of a scanner was burning into my brain. It started to feel like I might be stuck doing this for the rest of my life.

After some time passed, though, things started to shift. My contract was extended, I was given additional responsibilities, and my pay increased. Sure, it still wasn't my dream job or in the ideal line of work I hoped for, but it definitely made my days in the meantime significantly more tolerable—even interesting. Those shifts sparked momentum and motivation. I was eventually able to talk to some of the leaders at the advertising agency that was the main tenant of the building and make some connections there. I would use those conversations to secure a conversation with another marketing firm in town that eventually led to an interview and a job offer there. I was on the way to a career in the field I desired. It took perseverance, though. I had to pay my dues and I had to make something happen.

—Whitney H., Small-Business Owner

MIDDLE OF THE FUNNEL:

FEELINGS AND EXPERIENCES FURTHER INTO YOUR CAREER

5
I Feel Like I Am Buried in Work—and My Job Is Throwing Dirt on My Head

Just as there is a Line of Boredom, there is also the opposite. The opposite is when you feel as if you are buried in work. No, actually it feels as if you are buried in work and your job is standing on the ground above you, drinking a beer with its foot on your head laughing at you while you flail in the dirt. Yes, this happens too.

THE LINE OF MAXIMUM CAPABILITY

When you feel this way, you have reached the Line of Maximum Capability. This line represents the highest Degree of Stretch for you in a job, given your skills, knowledge, and experience. If your job is beneath the Line of Maximum Capability, generally you feel fairly confident you can do your job well and not screw up too often. When your job jumps above your Line of Maximum Capability, the emotional shit hits the fan. Above the LMC is where you start feeling overwhelmed. As in crushed, buried, flailing. I describe these types of situations in more detail in chapter 7. First, though, I want to explore how the Line of Maximum Capability changes over time.

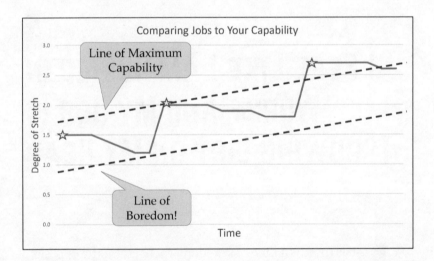

Typically, you stay well below the LMC in your first job. Entry-level jobs tend to be fairly easy, as we discussed, so you may never reach that point. The second job may creep up toward the LMC, especially in the beginning when you are faced with tasks or responsibilities that are new to you. Often, about the third job is when you really start to have the most LMC risk. That's typically when you have been promoted or moved upward in your profession and you now have larger responsibilities. These new responsibilities may include being held accountable for a budget of a department or leading a team of people. At this point in your career, just about every job you will have will bounce above and below the LMC at different times. The further you advance in your career, the more often and longer duration you will have above your LMC. (If this doesn't happen, then the monkey will come back to visit you and you will make changes to avoid the LOB.)

Notice that over time your LMC increases. This means you can handle harder and more complex situations because you have experienced hard and complex situations already in your career. The next time you experience a similar situation, you will know how to handle it and the situation will stay below your Line of Maximum Capability.

> **Something I have learned:** Over the long term, the way you move up your Line of Maximum Capability is to put yourself in challenging situations that help you develop new skills and enhance your capabilities.

Almost every one of my jobs has pushed me above my LMC. The reasons have varied. It may have been that I was too focused on the tactical work and didn't realize that the work environment was changing on me. I may have been heads down on the work but didn't realize the implications of adding several new clients. Or it may have been that I didn't plan appropriately for a key person on my team leaving the company. One memorable point in my career was with Dollar General. A small group of employees had been chosen to work on a special project to improve the way our stores operated, and I was among those chosen. Being part of this group was a pivotal moment in my career. However, it also was a catalyst for some serious LMC stress.

Our group was paired with a team of consultants from McKinsey Consulting. For those of you who have not worked with McKinsey before, these people are for real. They are smart and analytical with strong interpersonal and communication skills. If the project requires working all night, they just roll up their sleeves and work all night. I like to think I have a strong work ethic and consider myself reasonably intelligent, but at that point in my career working with these folks was uncharted territory for me. We were traveling every week to Texas to work five days nonstop on the project. The work we were doing was highly variable in nature and had absolutely no playbook. We were testing and building and creating new business processes in a rapid manner with high expectations from the C-suite of the company on our deliverables. And we were given a lot of autonomy. In previous work experiences, when I really did not know what I was doing, I had always been able to figure things out faster than my manager expected. In this role, though, I was clearly above my LMC. I was working really long hours during the day and into the evening, then going back to the hotel room at night to review fifty-plus emails, and then work on project update documents and PowerPoint presentations late into the night. At the end of the week, I would go home, do laundry, and then turn right around to pack again and head back to the airport on Monday morning. The work was incredibly stimulating, but I was also getting dumped on by the dirt.

> ***Something I have learned:*** *The two-sided nature of stimulating jobs is that they are always bouncing you up against the LMC. Your ability to stay sane depends on how long the periods are when you are above the LMC or how often the situations are when you are above the LMC.*

In this role, I was at or above the LMC for six months. It was not the technical nature of the work that overwhelmed me but the pace and volume of that work. My manager at the time knew the workload was crushing me, and he did one of the most infuriating (at the time) yet effective management tactics I have ever experienced. He asked me to meet him in our workroom at the hotel, where he and the lead McKinsey guy were waiting. He then asked me how things were going, and I don't remember exactly how I replied but I must have implied that the pace was intense. He handed me a marker and asked me to go up to the whiteboard and list the categories of items I was working on. He then asked me to write next to each category an estimate of the percentage of my time that area was consuming. I was totally caught off guard and stumbled through a handful of items with my best estimate of the percentage. When I stepped back and looked over my estimates, I saw that my total percentage added up to less than 100 percent. I started to go back and increase the percentages of some of the work areas, but he stopped me and said I couldn't do that. He then asked why I felt so overwhelmed if I wasn't even using 100 percent of my work capacity or time.

You know those moments where it seems as if you can feel the blood building up from your feet, up through your legs, up your torso, and it is going to blow out of the top of your head? This was one of those times.

Who the fuck are you to question what I am doing? Are you fucking serious? I have been busting my ass on this project with no help at all. I am putting in consecutive sixteen-hour days and sleep about five hours a night. My wife has forgotten what the hell I look like. We stay in this shitty hotel every damn week, and all you do is dump more and

*more work onto us. I don't have a goddamn extra minute
to spare, so I frankly don't give a shit what I wrote on this
board. My ass is full of fucking work, so back the hell off!*

That is what I was saying in my head as I stood in front of them
and clenched my fists open and closed. It was the angriest I have
ever been at a manager in my career. I do know that I dropped one
f-bomb on him, but we were also personal acquaintances before
work colleagues, so he let it pass with only a slight comment later.
The moment, however, was also one of the most motivating points
in my career. He absolutely knew I was using 100 percent of my
time, but he was also making a profound but glaringly obvious
point that I was way over my LMC and didn't know why. That
shit-ass moment with my manager made me resolute that I would
never, *ever* be susceptible to not knowing where I was spending my
time again. I am incredibly appreciative to that manager for setting
in motion what has become years of improvement in personal
productivity, which we will cover in the next chapter.

Before we get to that, it is valuable to look at the reasons your
job will get above the LMC. There are three:

1. You don't have the technical knowledge or skills to do
   the job.
2. The pace of the job is more than you can handle.
3. Occasionally, something comes along out of the blue
   that just absolutely blows up your job.

It is rare to have a job without having the required technical
skills to complete that job. That thing called the hiring process typically filters out unqualified people. If you happen to be in a position and you don't actually know how to do most of what is being
asked of you and you are generally expected to be able to do the

work on your own, then someone likely screwed up an interview with you. Again, these instances are rare. Not being able to keep up with the pace of your work is likely the most common reason that your job jumps your LMC. This was most definitely the case for my six months in Texas.

> **Something I have learned:** *If your job puts you above your LMC for too long, you run the risk of either burning out and quitting or failing to the point that you are fired.*

Neither of these is a positive outcome. To keep the number and duration of spikes above the LMC manageable, you need to improve your technical knowledge, increase your productivity, or reduce your workload.

To improve your technical knowledge, you need to first ask for help, and the best place to start is your manager. This sounds tricky, as you don't want your manager to feel you are incapable of doing your job. In the same way that we prepared our Skit in chapter 2, you will want to prepare a kind of script for this conversation with your manager. Do not go in unprepared. You need to be able to explain your position with insight and confidence. Before the conversation, ask yourself the following questions about your job:

> ➤ **Which parts of your job do you know how to do well? Where do you have sufficient knowledge to be successful in your job? What are some recent examples of how you did these parts of your job effectively?** Answering these questions should be easy, as you know what you are good at doing.

> ➢ **Where are you struggling? What specific aspects or tasks are you not capable of doing to the level of excellence you desire? What are some recent examples of these points of struggle?** Answering these questions also should be easy, as you know when you are failing.

> ➢ **What skills or knowledge do you think you need to be able to lower your LMC and find more success?** This question may be a little more difficult, as you may not know what you don't know. Think specifically what went wrong during points of struggle for you. Is it a leadership gap? A technology skill gap? Industry knowledge gap?

> ➢ **If you had to develop a plan to close the gap you have with these skills and experiences, how would you do it?** This may be the hardest question to answer, as you may not know how to go about getting this skill or knowledge. Consider actions such as finding a mentor who excels at your gap areas, job-shadowing someone who is good at the specific work, or taking a class in that particular area.

> ➢ **How long do you think it will take you to acquire these skills or knowledge?** Do your best to estimate based on your own intuition. There is no perfect answer here.

Once you have answered these questions, you now have a script to use for the conversation with your manager. She likely already knows you are above your LMC, or she will eventually. Schedule a specific time to talk with her. In this meeting, use your script to explain that you are struggling in your job and that you want to be successful. Describe with candor where you think you are succeeding, where you are struggling and why, what the gaps are that you have identified, and your ideas on how to close those gaps. Ask if she is willing to work with you to make your plan happen. Most reasonable managers will be surprised and then supportive of an employee who comes to them so proactively. If she is not willing to help you with the plan, then you may be in a position that is not sustainable long term and you should consider finding a new role.

If your job has you above your LMC for an extended period of time for the other two reasons—because you can't keep up with the pace of the work or something unusual has come along and wreaked havoc on your job—then chapters 6 and 7 will help you. Overall, expect to be challenged in your career. The Line of Maximum Capability is your friend, but only if you can give yourself enough space to acknowledge what is happening and why.

6

I FEEL LIKE I CAN'T GET ANY WORK DONE

Almost all of us have those times when we feel like we just cannot keep up with our work. The inbox fills up faster than we can empty it. The day gets full of meetings and there is no time to actually get things done other than nights and weekends. There seems to be no end in sight to the pace of work and we just cannot catch a break. Yet again, we want to run far away. This is an absolutely common feeling, and there is a solution. Once you see and experience the solution, it will be so obvious to you that you will wonder why you didn't think of it before.

RECURRING AND NONRECURRING WORK

In most companies, there are three types of work: recurring work, nonrecurring work, and meetings/conference calls. Recurring work is when you do essentially the same activities throughout the day, day after day. This type of work is usually more tactical than strategic and usually happens in entry-level positions. My first job at Dollar General was filled primarily with recurring work. Every day, I used a software system to create combinations of shipments to generate truckloads of merchandise. I worked with five other people who did the exact same job. All day, we would use the same software system to create and send these truckloads. Right click, add, right click. Scroll down. Right click, add, right click. Scroll down. Over and over. At the end of the day, we knew we were finished because there were no more shipments to create. The list was empty. Overnight, however, the merchandising team across the hall would have placed a bunch of new orders, and all of those orders would be pushed into our logistics system. Each morning, there was a new batch of orders to be worked, so we would right click, add, right click again through those orders. This is recurring work. As an employee of recurring-work jobs, you will likely only spend a small amount of your time and energy thinking about how to improve the process of the work, how to do the same work for less cost, and how to improve the operation of the work. You only spend a small amount of time doing this because you are too busy doing the recurring work of right click, add. Additionally, most of the thinking and planning and improving is being done by your supervisor instead of you. She spends probably half of her time doing recurring work (although different than yours) and the rest of the time doing nonrecurring work, which is the second type of work.

Nonrecurring work usually starts to be part of your job once you move above entry-level positions. It includes tasks such as leading initiatives or projects, improving processes, measuring the performance of a group of employees or a department, dealing with employee needs and issues, planning for future growth or changes in the business, or reducing the costs of the way work is done. Think about these activities as the building, creating, or improving of business. The higher your role is in the company, the more nonrecurring work you do and the less recurring work you do. The CEO of a company does no recurring work. None. Everything a CEO does and faces each day is different from all of the days before, forever. Different decisions, different problems, different activities. It makes sense that the shift in the ratio of recurring to nonrecurring work parallels your journey "up" the company.

The third type of work is meetings. As an entry-level employee, you may only participate in a few meetings each week or month. At my first position at Dollar General, I think I only participated in maybe one meeting every week or every other week. That's it. The purpose of this meeting was to get the six of us who did the same job together with our boss, the supervisor, to talk about how we were doing with our recurring work. In this meeting, we covered topics such as how fast were we working, what was not working well, and what was working well. If we worked forty hours a week on average, we only spent one hour of those total forty hours in meetings. The other thirty-nine hours were spent on recurring work. As with nonrecurring work, the higher up you get in a company, the more meetings you have. This is because meetings are used to discuss nonrecurring work. The CEO of a company spends almost all of his time in meetings discussing nonrecurring work (such as initiatives, strategies, or projects) or the measurement of recurring work (such as sales, productivity, or cost).

My point in all of this is that usually when you move into positions that have more nonrecurring work, you experience instances and situations that put you above your Line of Maximum Capability. Why? Because nonrecurring work is highly variable and unpredictable, so it is hard for your boss to know how much of it you can handle.

> *Something I have learned:* When you combine a bunch of nonrecurring work with a bunch of meetings, the wheels can quickly come off the cart.

That's when you feel like you are buried. Your day is filled with meeting after meeting. When you are not in meetings, you can hear your inbox filling up with emails from other nonrecurring-work people asking you to solve problems or build or create or improve something. The emails are sucking the life out of your future nights and weekends. When you get above the LMC, you start taking your phone to the bathroom with you so you can knock out a few emails. You start multitasking in meetings instead of listening. Work-life balance becomes a distant dream. I would guess that most people who are in middle management (people in nonrecurring-work jobs) live in a constant state of feeling overwhelmed with work. It is a crippling feeling that sabotages our lives both inside and outside of work. The feeling sneaks into our suitcases when we pack for vacation and then jumps out two days into our trip and tells us to check in on emails. I don't think we understand the emotional or psychological implications of spending a career in this mode of work fluidity. We are the first generation to exist with the ability to work anywhere and anytime. It's not good.

How do we deal, then? What is the solution? I have a theory that I have tested many times, at many different companies. The theory is this: if you walk in the door of any random company at 8:00 a.m., go into the office of any random middle manager, and ask that employee this very simple question—"Two hours from now, at 10:00 a.m. TODAY, if you are not in a meeting, what task or initiative are you going to be working on?"—that middle manager will not be able to answer you. Again, I have tested this theory many times, and no employee has ever known or been able to answer my question. What I mean by this is that *none* of the people I have ever asked could tell me what they would be doing specifically two hours from that moment. By specifically, I mean none of them could tell me which business initiative, task, or piece of work they would be doing in two hours.

None!

Zero!

Ever!

That's really fucked up.

Now, think about this for a second. Companies are complex organizations that depend on many moving parts to make them work. Companies are led by middle managers and senior managers who are well compensated to make decisions, operate, sell, improve, and analyze. Why on earth does NOBODY know what they are going to be doing in two hours? How *is* that? And more importantly, why is that acceptable?!

Think about this parallel. If you have kids who are in school, you can follow this example. If you don't have kids, imagine that you do. Let's say you walk your son to his classroom one morning. When you get to the door of the class, you see the teacher smiling, and you ask this very simple question: "Teacher! What are you going to do today in class?"

Imagine if she responded, "I am not sure! I am going to just see what is happening throughout the day and go from there!"

Huh? You would probably think, *What the hell kind of school is this? What is this teacher thinking? She doesn't have any idea or lesson plan for what she is doing today? What are my education dollars going toward anyway?* You would freak. You would absolutely freak, and you would storm down the hall into the principal's office and demand better from your son's teacher.

So why don't managers know what they will they be doing throughout the day? Why is this total lack of planning acceptable? Additionally, why don't these people's bosses or managers know this is the state of their managers' work habits? The answer is actually very simple. Their bosses are using their time in exactly the same way! In fact, almost all nonrecurring workers in every company are using their time this way. So how are people using their time? How are they working? This question is one of the most interesting and simple, yet also one of the most complex aspects of the modern workforce. Whenever I dissect it with people, they can't understand how they didn't see it before.

THE SOURCES AND CHANNELS OF YOUR WORK

Work can come to you from several different sources. Your manager might ask you to do a specific task or project in a one-on-one meeting. A customer might ask you to do something for them on a client call. You might think of something you need to do. A work colleague might suggest that you take on a specific task in a group meeting. Your company might have specific actions that are required at different times during the year such as performance reviews. Your job description might include specific tasks. Your recurring or nonrecurring work can originate from any of these places on any given day.

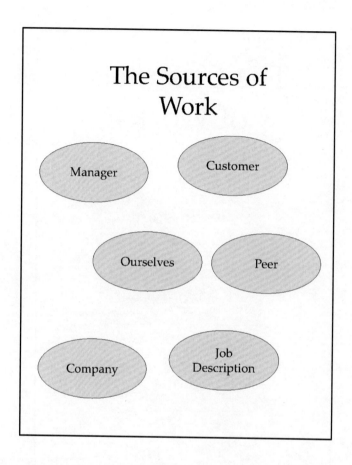

The channels of work are the ways in which you receive the work. These channels include verbally being asked to do something in a meeting or phone call, written via an email, mentally via a thought you have yourself, or perhaps through a technology system you use that simply feeds you work tasks.

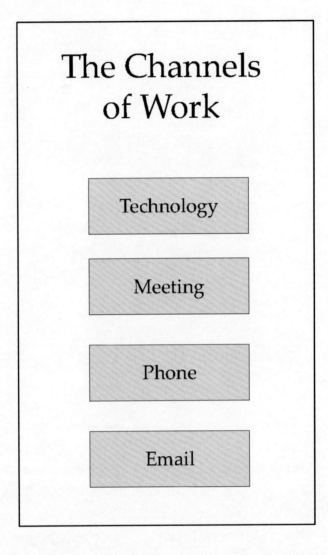

The Channels
of Work

Technology

Meeting

Phone

Email

If you observe most middle-management employees and above, you will see two main uses of their time: meetings and email. Companies have been conducting lots of meetings for a long time, so this aspect is not new. What is new is the use of scheduling-technology programs, such as Outlook, which allow meetings to be scheduled openly and freely by anyone. It is likely that we have more meetings now than we used to because they are easier to schedule. That's one thing to consider, yet it is not meetings that are causing the problem.

The other aspect to consider is email. Email is fairly new as it relates to the modern workforce. Many middle managers and above receive fifty to a hundred work emails a day. Some of them are relevant to them, some are communications to everyone, and some are just copies to a group. We can't help but feel mentally and emotionally pulled to check these emails. When we do so, we feel as if we are accomplishing work. The problem, though—and this is a very important distinction—is that *the modern manager actually looks to their email inbox as the primary source of their "work."* Some of our most important employees are looking to their emails to tell them what to do. I can't overemphasize how illogical and ill-informed this practice is. Yet email is also not the source of the problem.

> **Something I have learned:** *If you look to email as the source of your work, you are letting others prioritize your time, your focus, and your initiatives.*

The source of the problem is that you have lost control of your prioritization process for your nonrecurring work. Instead, you are delegating your work to everyone who sends you an email, and none of those people have insights into your priorities or your goals for the day, the month, the quarter, or the year. Only *you* do! Yet if you delegate your primary source of work to meetings and emails, you are actually never stepping back and prioritizing your nonrecurring work. You go from one meeting to another, and when you are not in meetings, you go back to your desk, open your email, and see what waits for you. You dive into the tasks that have recently shown up that may seem urgent or that you feel you can complete quickly. You get a little shot of dopamine, and then you move on to the next meeting or the next email. Do you see what is missing? This way of working is incredibly reactionary, and therefore doesn't allow you to work on the important initiatives or tasks that will advance the business forward. These important activities actually constitute your nonrecurring work!

In this reactionary mode, you only get to these more critical bodies of work either when your boss asks you for an update or when you are given a deadline. Because you are not completing your nonrecurring work, you don't ever feel organized or "on top of things." Instead, you feel anxious, and everything around you feels chaotic and out of your control. I know this intimately, as I used to work in this same way. I never felt calm. I never felt confident. I never felt that I could let my guard down.

> **Something I have learned:** *You can get more work done if you actually know what you are going to do with your time. Duh. Sorry, but duh.*

In fact, you can run freaking circles around yourself when you actually know what you are going to do. I didn't start out my career with this knowledge, I had to learn it the hard way. However, I have spent the past fifteen years developing and refining a different way to work. This is not just about managing email. Email management is a component, but the overarching foundation of the work method is simply *to plan every minute of every day*. That's right. At the beginning of every day, you have to know what you are going to do all day *in detail*.

No Plan for Our Day

One phenomenon that has significantly influenced the way we work is our use of online calendars. If you really think about it, your calendar drives much of how you approach your workday. The visual below is an example of what a Monday–Friday calendar looks like for the vast majority of nonrecurring-work employees.

What do you see?

The days are composed of a lot of meetings, which is not unusual, as meetings are a requirement of nonrecurring work. The more striking observation is the white space in between the meetings. What do you see there?

Look closely.

What is in this white space?

Nothing!

That's correct, nothing! Nothing is in there! There is nothing in all of this open time! Not a damn thing! So what do you do during this white space?

If you were physically to follow the employee of this calendar around an office watching him throughout the day, you would likely see him leave these meetings, go back to his desk, and dive into the email pile. Approximately ten minutes before the next meeting, the calendar system would pop an alert, and he would get up to go to the next meeting. Eventually, with enough force from his manager for a deadline, the employee would actually work on a specific initiative or task. This calendar and work method is what a week looks like that is not in his control.

If this is your work process, when do you work on actual "work"? By "work" I mean the near-term tasks and initiatives that managers are responsible for accomplishing: proposals, performance monitoring, performance reviews, budget analysis, presentations, solution innovation, and all the other unique tasks that are driven by the business. These initiatives are the core improvement engine of all business. They are what help companies maintain a competitive advantage, increase revenue, evolve, and satisfy customers. So when does this work occur? When do you do this stuff?

And more importantly, *why can't we see it on anyone's calendar?*

The reason we can't see it on anyone's calendar is that almost no one is planning when they will do this work. No one says to themselves, "I need to create this PowerPoint presentation for the finance department for my budget for next year, and I am going to do this work tomorrow at 10:00 a.m." Almost no one is working this way. We are not prioritizing and planning our work at nearly the frequency or level of detail that we need to in order to maximize our personal output.

The result is the intersection of two very damaging practices. The first is using up your valuable white space without any specific purpose, and the second is failing to plan for when to do your nonrecurring work. You are wasting your white space and you are neglecting your nonrecurring work. This combination makes you feel like crap. It makes you feel scattered, anxious, and worried. It also significantly reduces your productivity, and you are one of the employees whom the company has put in charge of running the improvement engine of the company. My personal estimation is that this combination puts a 15 to 20 percent drag on the output of the most essential employees of a company. For the CFOs out there, imagine getting a 15 to 20 percent reduction in your management costs. Or said another way, imagine being able to grow another 15 to 20 percent in revenue without adding a single manager because you could absorb all the new work associated with that growth with your existing staff.

There is absolutely a better way to work. A system that enables nonrecurring-work employees to advance the critical business-building initiatives at a faster pace. A method that requires less supervisor interaction. A practice that requires fewer status-update meetings. Most importantly, a way of working that allows you to go home in the afternoon and let it go and enjoy your life outside of the office.

Imagine walking into any company's office at 8:00 a.m. and stopping in the office of any manager and asking him the question, "What you are going to do today?" Now imagine the person answering you in this way:

From 8:00 to 9:00, I am going to check and reply to emails and voicemails.

From 9:00 to 10:00, I will be in a meeting to discuss top sales prospects.

From 10:00 to 11:00, I am going to work on my end-of-the-year performance reviews.

From 11:00 to 11:30, I am going to check and reply to emails and voicemails.

From 11:30 to 12:00, I am going to eat lunch.

From 12:00 to 1:00, I will be in a meeting to discuss account-management staffing.

From 1:00 to 2:00, I will be in a meeting to discuss implementation of our next client.

From 2:00 to 3:00, I am going to work on a presentation for the strategy retreat.

From 3:00 to 3:30, I am going to prepare for our team meeting tomorrow.

From 3:30 to 4:30, I will be in a meeting to discuss budget for next year.

From 4:30 to 5:00, I am going to check and reply to emails and voicemails.

From 5:00 to 5:15, I am going to plan what I will do tomorrow.

If someone answered your question in this manner, you would be astonished. You would freak. You just would. This answer is possible, though. You can achieve this type of workload management, and when you do, you will wonder how you ever existed in any other way.

There are three critical components to this work model:

1. Having a digital "One Place" for all nonrecurring work to be organized.
2. Investing ten minutes daily on prioritization of that nonrecurring work.
3. Designating specific nonrecurring work on the calendar during specific times of the day.

A DIGITAL ONE PLACE

Nonrecurring-work employees are constantly bombarded with new tasks, initiatives, activities, and to-dos. The sources of these tasks, requests, and to-dos vary but are finite. As we discussed, often they arrive from bosses via email or verbal requests. Sometimes they arise in meetings as assignments employees give themselves. Other times individuals just think of things they need to do. But where do these items go? How do they translate from an idea or a request to an action item? From my observations, one of several things happens. Employees either write these items down in a paper notebook, attempt to mentally commit them to memory, maybe they put them into an Excel file, and a very few will put them into a technology system like Evernote. None of these methods is effective, though. They are all flawed because they don't allow employees to see their tasks in aggregate or in order of priority, both of which are critically important.

Imagine you go to twenty different meetings over a week's time. In each meeting, you are assigned three tasks. You write these tasks in a notebook during each meeting. You have a list from each meeting, and all of these lists are therefore in sequential order of the date of the meetings. These notes are now separated over many pages, and it is very difficult to see the sum total of all the work in a holistic manner. To see all the tasks holistically that you need to do that originated in all these meetings, you have to flip through many different pages in a notebook that potentially could go back days or even weeks. Alternatively, you would need to continue to rewrite in your notebook a new consolidated list every day of only the open items. Neither of these is an efficient or sustainable way of looking at all the work to be done in an aggregate way.

Additionally, initiatives or tasks are usually not completed in one effort. It normally takes several different points of effort to complete an initiative. You may start an initiative and then need to "park" it until you can work on it at another time. If you advance an initiative but do not finish the task and you want to write a note reminding you of the next action to take on the initiative, there usually isn't space in a notebook where the original task was written to add comments.

For example, if you work on a presentation but need to remember that you emailed someone for information and need to follow up on that email in three days, there physically is not a place to write that reminder down next to the original task. So how do you remember in three days to check to see if you have received that information? Where does that reminder exist that is associated with that initiative? Typically, nowhere. Individuals just randomly remember at some point in the future that they emailed someone for information, but it may be a week later or a month later. Meanwhile, the pace of the completion of the task has slowed and was not in the individual's control.

These same problems apply to fluid technology tools, such as Evernote. Evernote is great for logging thoughts and notes, but it does not allow an *aggregate* view of specific tasks, the status of the tasks, and the time frame for when you want to work on them next.

> **Something I have learned:** *To get to the place where you can prioritize your work, you first need to be able to see all of your nonrecurring work in aggregate.*

To see all your nonrecurring work in aggregate, you need a "One Place" that is better than paper or memory. If you are someone who likes to write tasks in a notebook, that is a reasonable starting point for your work-management process. However, on at least a daily basis, it is essential to transcribe these items from paper into a digital One Place. There are hundreds of tech applications that allow you to store tasks, assign a category, put comments on the task, attach documents to the task, and monitor a due date. (I use one called Asana, as it does all of these features, and it is free for the basic version.) The critical benefit of this One Place is that you can see everything you have to do all in one place. Hence the brilliant name, One Place.

Most initiatives or tasks take several distinct efforts to complete. A presentation may require several versions. A project or initiative will take several steps. An essential part of the One Place is to use the "due date" feature in a unique way. Most people think of the "due date" as the final date that an initiative is due. However, I suggest using the due date as the date you want to work on the initiative next. Imagine one of your nonrecurring work items is to create a presentation for a new customer. You will need to get information from several different people, organize and compile that information, have the presentation reviewed and approved, and get printed copies made. Imagine you work on a first draft of the presentation but you need your boss to review it, so you email it to him. Based on the date of the meeting with the customer, you judge that you need your boss to review the document within three days from now. Your due date for this presentation task should be three days from now (when you need to receive it back from your boss). You want to use the due date as a reminder for yourself to advance the task to the next step. Without this next step–based due date, you will be dependent on someone else to do what you need them to do, or you will be dependent on you to remember to check back with that person. Both of these dependencies put your success at risk. However, if you use the due date based on the next milestone of the task, then in three days from now, you will know to reach out to your boss to ensure he is finished reviewing. You will have structurally ensured your success, as the technology will tell you when and what to do next. Another example would be that you worked on the presentation but ran out of time, and you want to remind yourself to work on it again two days from now. You can either hope you remember to work on it (behavior-dependent and risky) or you can tell yourself you want to work on it in two days by setting a due date in your One Place of two days from now (structural and not risky). In essence, the due date is you telling yourself when you next want to work on an initiative to ensure it gets done. Imagine all of your work initiatives and tasks are managed this way so every task has a continuously evolving due date. Using the due date as a reminder to advance the task to the next step ensures you are in control of the process.

Within the aggregate view of the One Place, you can see both notes you have made on a task in the past and deadlines for action items in the future. This aggregated view is critical for the next step, which is a daily ten-minute investment in prioritization.

DAILY PRIORITIZATION

Prioritization simply means looking at all your nonrecurring work and deciding which tasks you want to work on in the near future. This practice sounds easy but is an incredibly difficult behavior to adopt. I have been doing this practice for years and it is still difficult for me. The reason it is difficult is that we don't usually associate planning with productivity. Planning doesn't actually accomplish anything on our to-do lists, so we are reluctant to value it. It is critical to understand this mental block, though, and overcome it.

> **Something I have learned:** *If you want to kick ass at productivity tomorrow, you have to kick ass at prioritizing and planning today.*

Prioritization is the last mile, the holy grail. It involves first selecting and then placing chosen tasks into your online calendar daily. If you do everything up to this point but fail to load your prioritized and planned activities into your calendar, you are going to miss most of the benefit.

When you have a One Place, Daily Prioritization takes only about ten minutes, and yet this step is where most people struggle because it requires establishing a new pattern of behavior. As such, an important step of Daily Prioritization is actually putting the task of prioritization and planning itself on the online calendar. Yes, I mean plan time to plan time! You need to create an actual recurring fifteen-minute task on your calendar at the end of every workday and label it "Work Planning." If this activity is on your calendar and the reminder pops up every day, you will be much more likely to do it.

Let's imagine it is 5:00 p.m. and your calendar pops a reminder for "Work Planning." Fortunately, throughout the day and the week, you have been moving tasks from your notebook into your One Place so you have a single place to access all the nonrecurring work you have accumulated or been assigned. To plan how you will use tomorrow's time, you simply open your One Place and quickly look through all the activities. Based on what you know is important at the current point in time, you select the tasks you want to work on the next day. If you are wondering, *How much time will I have tomorrow to work on this stuff?* you are right on track with your question, so stay with me.

If you stopped here with this process, you would be light-years ahead of most employees. However, you would still likely fail at getting those tasks done. The reason you would fail is that you have not gotten to the last mile, which is to assign a specific time in the day (tomorrow) when you want to work on each specific task. Without this step, you would fall back into the same routine of meetings and emails, and at the end of the day, you would not have advanced the nonrecurring work items you identified the day before.

PLAN EVERY MINUTE

The third step brings it all home. And this is where people think you are crazy. You have your One Place open in front of you *and* you have your online work calendar open in front of you. These two items represent the supply of work and the available time to process the work. The last step is to bring these two areas together. When you look at your calendar, you will see meetings and white space. The white space is the time for getting shit done.

But wait! I know what many of you are thinking right now. You are thinking, *If I look at my calendar at the end of the day, I won't have ANY open time tomorrow, as all of my time will already be booked by meetings!* Yes, this is a common phenomenon. Many of us do not have much—or any—time outside of meetings when looking a few days into the future. Why? Because with open-calendar systems, other people can freely schedule meetings for us. When we lose control of our calendars, we lose control of our time.

> *Something I have learned:* You must be selfish with your time!

Yes, selfish. Your time is *your* time. Your day is *your* day. If your days are normally filled with meetings that either you or others schedule and you therefore never have time to work on nonrecurring work, then you need to be more selfish with your time and therefore more selfish with your calendar. To be selfish with your time and calendar is actually very simple.

First, you need to tackle the way you manage email. After years of the endless inbox, I have figured out how to dominate emails. Reference the calendar snapshot below and you will notice something unique. There are specific times during the day for emails and phone calls. Yes, this actually means you schedule specific times during the day to check and reply to emails.

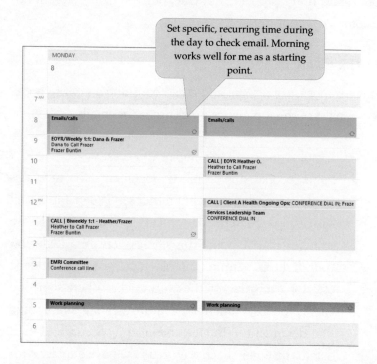

Typically I schedule time to check emails for one hour in the morning, generally for thirty minutes before lunch, again for thirty minutes after lunch, and then at the end of the day. For the morning email slot, I set a recurring appointment every day so that time is reserved forever on my calendar. When it is not one of those set times, I don't check email. Easier said than done! Email is like a drug. It is almost impossible to resist. If you try to leave your email system open while focusing on your nonrecurring-work blocks, you will fail. Spoiler alert! The lure of email will be too strong and you will want to glance, *just to see* how many have arrived, and you will get sucked into an email vortex. You will not come out of this vortex until your next meeting, and you will have completely lost that dedicated time and your nonrecurring work will be incomplete. Your boss will hate you and everyone will laugh at you. Okay, that's probably not true, but you definitely will not have completed your task.

TAME THE EMAIL BEAST

Email is a beast of a topic and could consume an entire book, so here is a list of the top tactics for clearing out emails:

> ➤ Unsubscribe to all the crap as you get it.
> ➤ Some people don't embed documents for meetings inside a calendar invite but rather send a separate email with the document for a meeting. These people are strange. To overcome this silliness, create a folder on your desktop. Within that folder, create five subfolders, one for each day of the workweek. When someone emails you a document for a future meeting, simply drag that document to the day the meeting occurs and then delete the email. Each day, you now have a folder with all of the documents for your meetings and all those emails are gone.
> ➤ Delegate like crazy.

> ➢ Don't set response requests for the meetings you schedule.
> ➢ If you travel a lot, create a folder called "airplane" on your desktop and drop any documents into this folder that you want to review on the airplane in case there is no Wi-Fi. Delete the email that had the document in it.

My observations of twenty years of email use have taught me the following lessons. Every time I checked an email while trying to work on an important piece of nonrecurring work, not only did I lose the time I spent responding to that email, I also lost the time it took me mentally to get back to the same depth of thought I had before I checked the email. I estimate it takes me two minutes to ramp back up to whatever I was doing. If you have an hour of blocked time and you check six emails during that hour, with each email consuming one minute, you will lose six minutes working on the emails—but you will also lose twelve minutes mentally "recovering" from working on each email. So during that hour of time you set aside, you actually lose eighteen minutes to email. You are only getting to use 80 percent of every hour. At the end of the hour, you haven't finished your nonrecurring work, you are distracted, and you feel like crap.

The absolutely critical part of all of this stuff, and this is hard as shit to do, is actually to close down your email system while you do nonrecurring work. An unusually unknown fact is there is a secret hidden feature of email. This feature is designated by a small, lowercase black x in the upper right-hand corner of email systems. Very few modern-day employees know that if you click on this little black x, your email system actually closes out and goes away, leaving you with unfettered time to focus on important nonrecurring work. Okay, yes, I am being a total smartass, but this is what it takes. You actually have to close out of email. You have to. I have been doing this crap for years, and I still can't resist checking email when it is open. I have to close it out. You have to close it out. Do it. Another spoiler alert! This is really difficult to do. We are so connected to our email or Slack or whatever instant-messaging platform we use that we feel strange without them active. It is like standing in a forest all alone. Well, you are here to chop down some trees by not checking email throughout the entire day, so grab a damn axe and start chopping.

BLOCK AND TACKLE

Once you have established an effective way to manage email on your terms, you can move on to the second calendaring step, called Block and Tackle, which is to assign your actual work to a time slot on your calendar. If you typically have a lot of meetings that fill up your calendar, you will need to add a step to reserve future time for yourself, called Blocking. You just go into your calendar and look out a few days until you start to see some white space on your calendar where no meetings are scheduled. *Everyone* eventually has white space when you get far enough out. Once you start to find some white space, you simply go into your calendar and start to reserve blocks of time. I suggest blocking time across two consecutive days. How? Create fictional meetings or appointments with yourself on your calendar and marking them as "busy" in the calendar system. I actually type the word "Block" into these times.

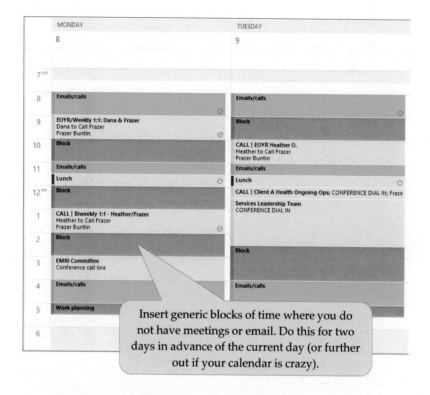

Insert generic blocks of time where you do not have meetings or email. Do this for two days in advance of the current day (or further out if your calendar is crazy).

You don't want to reserve an entire day, but perhaps two or three different blocks of time during each day. Mix up blocks of one hour and blocks of thirty minutes throughout the day (just name them "Block" for now), leaving some open space for meetings to be planned in the future. That way you have time reserved to do the work *you* want to do in the future. Once you get closer to those actual days, you will be very appreciative that you have blocked this time so you can actually get something accomplished! All you have to do then is use your fifteen minutes of work-planning time at the end of the day to look at your One Place, determine the important tasks, and put those specific tasks into the spaces on your calendar you previously called "Blocks." I actually mean taking one of the generic blocks and changing the word "Block" to the specific name of the task. If you have a thirty-minute block, you will want to find a task that you estimate will only take thirty minutes. If you have a two-hour block, you may want to split it up into two one-hour blocks for two different tasks. You can do this for one day out, two days out, three days out—whatever makes sense. The process is a daily recurring cycle of blocking generic time several days in advance and then converting generic blocks to specific tasks for tomorrow. Over and over!

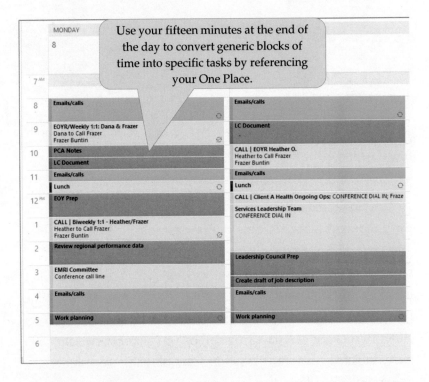

It's also a good idea to block time for lunch. If you don't, someone else will take it and you won't have time to eat, or you'll end up eating lunch in a meeting every day. Don't do that, because it sucks. Also, a best practice is to set your work tasks in a different color in your calendar. Outlook usually makes meetings light blue in color, so using a different color for emails, lunch, and nonrecurring work helps you look out across a day or a week and visually see the distribution of time across both meetings and tasks. I use green for emails and calls, orange for nonrecurring work tasks, and purple for out-of-the-office items.

So let's regroup on what you have done thus far. You have aggregated all your nonrecurring work into a digital One Place in a fluid manner on a daily basis. You have put a recurring ten- to fifteen-minute block of time on your calendar for the end of each day so you can prioritize what you want to work on the following day. You have pre-blocked time on your calendar so when you get to the end of the day, each day, you have generic blocks of time you can use to convert into actual, specific tasks for specific times in the day. You have also blocked time for checking and replying to emails. The result of all of these tactics is at the end of your planning time each day, you have a calendar for tomorrow that is completely full and in *your* control. There is no white space. There is no ambiguity. You know exactly what you are going to do when you walk in the office!

What does this do for you? From a productivity standpoint, you get more work done because you avoid incremental distractions. You are able to work on the tasks that are the most important because you have thought about those tasks and actively chosen them based on the current needs of the business. Emotionally, most of the anxiety around feeling overloaded and not sure if you are on top of things disappears. You can have confidence in the fact that you are working on the most important tasks because you believe in your process and you are in control. You can be better husbands and wives and parents and friends and individuals now outside of work. You can also chill the hell out!

YEP, THIS ACTUALLY WORKS

Now let's come back to the nay-sayers and the potential problems with this method of work.

What?

Seriously?

That's not possible.

That's a waste of time because my day will inevitably change.

I need to be responsive and accessible to my team by email all the time.

I have heard them all. Every reason why this method won't work. There is likely no reason you can come up with of why this concept will fail that I haven't already heard from someone when I first described this methodology to them. One of the biggest areas of pushback I receive is people telling me they don't have any time to do nonrecurring work because their day is full of meetings. Simple. Look far enough out and your calendar will eventually have white space. Block it before someone else does, and you will have time.

The other major pushback I hear is the argument that the workday is too variable. It changes all the time without any warning. This is likely true. Many people's days change all the time. Customers call, bosses give you unexpected work that is due immediately, fires erupt, last-minute meetings are scheduled. Sometimes small parts of our day change. Occasionally, an entire day blows up and everything changes. If our days might change, why go to all this work to plan things out? Aside from the intrinsic merits of implementing a system of organization and intentionality, the answer to this question relates to what you get in return for the effort required. Simply put, what is the return on investment of planning your day in a detailed manner? Let's consider the investment side. I have observed individuals assume this methodology and within their first week be able to plan their entire day in ten minutes. So ten minutes represents the investment of time or effort required. For the return side, I have personally quantified savings of 15 percent of my time from this methodology to do the same amount of work. Said another way, using this framework allows me to do 15 percent more work/output in the same amount of time. So on a weekly basis, I am investing ten minutes a day or fifty minutes a week of effort into daily planning, yet I receive four hundred fifty minutes of time back (assuming a fifty-hour workweek). Four hundred fifty minutes means I am getting an extra 1.5 hours per day. That is an incredible return on investment. I will take a ten-time return on anything, any day. I can then take that 1.5 hours and determine what I want to do with it. If I am getting crushed by my work and I am above the Line of Maximum Capability, I may give all of those 1.5 hours back to my personal life and bring my job down below my LMC. If I am not in that situation and I have created more available time during a normal workday, then I can backfill that available time with more work. Why on earth would anyone want to backfill available time with more work? If you enjoy your job and/or you want to advance your career, you can add more work, which will position you for a promotion or the opportunity to add skills or experiences.

> **Something I have learned:** *Even if you have a few catastrophic days of the week that completely blow up, the investment is still completely worth it.*

Another reason for pushback is that individuals, specifically managers, feel that they need to be extremely responsive to their staff members or customers. These managers feel they cannot be away from email because they need to be able to respond to their staff or customers immediately. This is a normal yet somewhat naïve management principle. Managers do not exist to serve every need of their staff instantly. Managers exist to establish the strategy, hire good people, monitor the behaviors, measure the results, and model the culture (as we will discuss in chapter 10). The most effective way for managers to assist staff members is to spend time in a productive manner to advance the department's critical business initiatives. Often, this means concentrating and producing deep work. Effective managers don't instantly respond to every email from their employees. Speed-to-response is not a gauge of a good manager. In fact, if a manager always responds instantly to his employees' emails, he likely is never working in deep concentration mode on business-advancing initiatives.

If you are a manager, it is a good idea to let your team know that you are switching to this methodology before going to it, especially if you have been someone who has responded instantly in the past. It will be helpful to explain why you are embracing this methodology and how it will benefit you and the group. You may be surprised at the number of people who are interested as well. I have had many people approach me in the office and ask if I have received an email they sent fifteen minutes ago because they now want to talk about it. When I respond that I only check email about three times a day, they look at my like I have two heads. It's funny.

Again, though, all of this work-method stuff is really difficult. Start slow and build up to it. Celebrate the small victories such as a day of actually closing out of email successfully during your work blocks. It is also important to realize that you will backslide and fail, so acknowledge those failures and don't beat yourself up. Just get back to the methods and keep trying. Once you build the habit, you will become dependent on it and will wonder how you ever worked successfully any other way. Completing your nonrecurring work at a rapid pace, you will absolutely see a difference in the quantity and quality of your work compared to your peers. More significantly, though, you will see a difference in the way you "show up" to work and life. In meetings, you will notice you are not as stressed out as most of the others. An aura of kickass productivity will surround you. See what you can do with this concept.

> *Throughout my career, there's always been more work to do than time in the workday. Early on, the solution was simple: get to the office earlier, stay later, or take work home if needed. That was okay for a while. My tasks were somewhat predictable. I was young, single, and had little on my personal schedule besides going to the gym and the occasional dinner with friends.*
>
> *As my career progressed and I moved into management roles, my workload increased and the type of work shifted. The routine tasks that I could just "grind out" became less and less of my job, and the demands on my time and attention became unpredictable. Now I had to react to requests from my boss, my boss's boss, my employees, clients, and board members. Everything seemed urgent and important. My workday was now spent in meetings and conference calls. I distinctly remember one workday consisting entirely of twelve consecutive conference calls scheduled back to back. As I looked at my calendar each morning, I felt a sense of dread. I knew the things I really needed to get done that day would have to be completed in the evening, taking away from time with my spouse and children. It felt like each workday was happening to me, instead of me controlling how my time was spent.*
>
> *When I was first introduced to the concepts of One Place, Block and Tackle, and Daily Prioritization, I was skeptical. I already knew what I had to do, I just didn't have any time to do it! How*

was this going to create time? But because I was buried and getting further buried with each day, I gave it a chance.

At the end of the first day, I added all my tasks into a One Place. All my tasks—work related or not. Surprisingly, that step alone made me feel a lot better. Everything that was rattling around in my mind or on some random page of a notepad was now in one place. Looking at my calendar for the next day, I could only find two thirty-minute slots to plug in tasks that were important to me. Only one hour! However, I looked out into next week, where my calendar was a bit less crowded, and I found more available time and blocked several hours to hold for future work. Over a week or two, the system really started to work. I was able to fill previously protected time blocks with the specific tasks that really mattered. My to-do list got shorter. Most importantly, I felt good about what I had accomplished each day and I felt in control.

Now, I'm not perfect. I slip out of the routine from time to time. And when I do, I'm quickly reminded by a sense of being overwhelmed that I need to reset myself, use my One Place, and schedule the work that really matters. When I do that, I'm right back in the driver's seat of my work life.

—Josh M., Principal Consultant

7
I Feel Like I Can't Handle This Situation

f you are pushing yourself in your career, you should have some major "Oh Shit" moments. These are situations that come out of nowhere and wreak havoc on your work life for a period of time. You will know if you've experienced one, or some, of these because they are the stuff of personal legend. They are the stories you tell your friends and family. If you haven't yet had any Oh Shit moments, just wait and you likely will.

You may be thinking, *But wait—we already talked about the Line of Maximum Capability.* Oh Shit moments are different than being above the LMC because they are typically one-off situations that don't repeat themselves on an ongoing basis. The good news is these tornadoes of frustration eventually track off and the dust settles. When you are in the middle of one, however, you feel way over your head and scared as crap. It absolutely sucks to feel this way, but these situations can help you develop skills that will serve you well in future crisis moments.

SHIT WILL HAPPEN

In my early thirties, I started a healthcare company by raising capital from a group of investors to purchase a small business. About five months into starting the company, the previous owner told my business partner and me that she was being investigated by the federal government for potential improper healthcare billing. For those of you who do not work in healthcare, the short version is that when the feds catch doctors and hospitals overcharging the government for healthcare services, typically some bad shit goes down. Our company got to experience some of that bad shit.

Whether this person actually did what the government accused her of doing is none of my business. She was an absolutely terrific clinician and a smart businessperson who helped a lot of people in her life. I don't know if she did or didn't do what the feds accused her of, but I do know that the situation rained down some holy chaos on my life for an entire year.

This was a major Oh Shit moment. Our company employed about fifteen nurse practitioners who provided healthcare services in nursing homes. All of these nurse practitioners were female and all of them reported to this senior nurse practitioner from whom we purchased the company.

She was their boss.

She was their hero.

She was their mentor.

She was their Santa Claus.

We had to fire Santa Claus.

And then we had to tell all our employees that Santa Claus was potentially going to prison.

If the employees all freaked out and quit, we were done. We would have had to close the business. As it stood, we had to go back to our investors—only five months into the existence of the business—and explain that the backbone of the company might be going away for a while, which in turn would probably negatively impact the potential success of the company.

> **Something I have learned:** *There will be times in your career when you feel like you are in way over your head and you are on the verge of failing at your job. You can make it through these times and learn a lot from these moments.*

As such, I was thrown way over my Line of Maximum Capability. Worse than that, I was on top of a painful Oh Shit spike. There was no one else above me to take over. There was no one else coming up with the plan. There was no one else deciding what to do. The inner dialogue in my head sounding something like the following:

> *I am underwater and my job as CEO is standing on the dock, beer in hand, saying, "Welcome to the CEO job, pal!" I wish someone else were the boss. I wish someone else could deal with this shit. What the fuck are we going to do? Is everyone going to quit? Yes, everyone is going to quit. Shit, shit, shit, shit, shit!*

CREATE SOME SPACE

What do you do here? One of the most important steps is to give yourself some space. Everything will feel urgent and critical, but it is extremely important not to rush into trying to solve the problem immediately. At these points in your career, you may be tempted to run into your boss's office or your colleague's office and "throw up" your feelings of being overwhelmed. It's okay to do this eventually, but first come up with a plan of what you think you should do to solve the problem at hand. To give yourself some space to create a plan, take a blank piece of printer paper and a pen and walk away from your desk. Leave your phone behind as well. Find an empty conference room or coffee shop corner and sit down with your pen and paper and just begin to write down whatever comes to mind as you think about the problem. You may first write down what the problem is, what is causing it, and what is making it even worse. Don't overthink this process. Just write down whatever comes to mind. It doesn't have to be complete sentences and can even just be a few words. Eventually, start to write down small parts of what could help solve the problem. Keep going. After a while, you will start to see the pieces of a potential solution come together. Flip the paper over and list three to five things in chronological order that you think could help start to solve the problem. This whole process will take about thirty minutes.

Then schedule time with your boss or colleagues to talk about the issue. When you talk with them, acknowledge that you are feeling buried and overwhelmed. Tell them you need their help figuring this out. Be a little bit vulnerable, as people will understand and respect you for putting yourself out there. Explain you have a recommendation or a starting point for a recommendation for how to get things back on track. You will be amazed at the organizational momentum you can inspire to fix an Oh Shit moment by using these tactics.

Another Oh Shit moment I experienced happened again at Dollar General, but this time when I was a buyer. In the retail industry, a buyer is someone who determines what products to sell in the stores, establishes relationships with companies who sell that stuff, negotiates a price, and allocates shelf space and store location for all the products. My role was as a buyer for home cleaning and paper products. One of the items I was responsible for was bleach. Yes, plain old household bleach. But here is the deal: we sold a crap-load of bleach. I mean a lot. We had nine thousand Dollar General stores, and each store sold about one hundred bottles a week, so that's roughly forty-seven million bottles of bleach per year. A lot of damn bleach.

One day I received a call from our store support center, which operated an inbound call center for store managers with a question or need. The support contact advised me that a store manager had called to report that several of her bleach bottles were swelling up and looked like they were going to burst. Hmmm, very strange. I called the store manager back, and sure enough, she said she had about twenty one-gallon plastic bottles of bleach that were totally swollen. As in they wouldn't even sit on the shelf because the bottoms were so rounded. I advised her to take the bottles off the shelf and put them in the supply room. A couple of hours later, I received another call from the call center stating a different store was reporting swollen bleach. Something was definitely happening. I called the vendor who made the bleach for us, and he assured me that this must be an isolated occurrence. I called the first store manager back, and she said the bottles were so swollen now that she feared they were going to explode. Oh crap. Exploding bleach bottles is not good for retail business. Exploding bleach bottles is literally the shit hitting the fan.

At this point, I was hanging in there, but I was twenty-six years old and had absolutely no experience to draw from. I was decent at solving problems, but this was pushing my limits. I knew I needed to get a message out to the stores so I could determine how widespread the problem was and develop a plan of action. I asked our IT department to broadcast a message out to all nine thousand stores advising any store manager that had swollen bleach bottles to leave me a voicemail on my office line. I then went to lunch.

After lunch I came back to my desk and noticed the light blinking on my phone, notifying me that I had a voicemail. Hmm. When I logged on to my phone, the message said, "You have 389 voicemails."

Oh shit. Oh shit. Oh shit. What have I done?!

My mind raced as I realized what I had done and what was about to happen to me. As fast as I could, I started writing down the store numbers and the number of bleach bottles each store reported as swollen. But meanwhile, more stores were using the phone system to dial directly into my voicemail. So in the time it took me to clear out one voicemail, I had twenty more waiting for me. More major shit. I felt like I couldn't handle the situation.

Over the next several months, I ended up having to coordinate a huge recall and reverse-logistics operation of thousands of swollen bleach bottles from random small towns across the country. Imagine trying to convince someone, *anyone*, to drive all over the United States to pick up swollen bleach bottles that look like they are going to burst and then put them in their car. There is no service for this. It just doesn't exist! The whole process was a huge debacle and had tons of mistakes along the way, but I eventually got it done. I learned a lot from this experience, both tactically and personally. I learned how to communicate with leaders within our company so they were confident I was managing the situation well. I learned how to manage a supplier who was responsible for selling us the bad bleach. I learned how to be creative and innovative to solve a problem. To be sure, I definitely didn't see any of these as learning opportunities during the actual experience. It was not until after the experience was over or maybe not even until the next wild shitshow I had to deal with that I realized how much I had actually learned from the situation.

These points in your career are absolutely terrible in the moment, especially when you first have them. You have no idea what to do, and you feel like you want to quit. As you experience more of these situations, however, you start to see them for what they are: a spike above your Line of Maximum Capability that will come back down to normal with time and problem solving. The more spikes you deal with, the more you learn about how to handle them and the more confident you become that you will get through them. The intensity will still be there, but you will be able to observe yourself feeling that way, which will give you the space you need to identify solutions and get things back on track.

8
WHAT THE HELL AM I DOING HERE?

Here" may be an actual place, or "here" may be a state of existence. "Hell" can take many different forms, but it's pretty much always hell. When a question has both "hell" and "here" in it, something crazy is usually going down.

This question will likely come to you when you are at the lowest of the low of whatever job you have at the time. It may be triggered by feeling really pissed off at having to travel to some random place, or it may be triggered by having to work during times when you don't think you should be, or by your boss who is an ass, or simply by the fact that you cannot do your job one more day. That feeling of wanting to flee will revisit you. You will wonder why this stuff happens to you and never to any of your friends. You will question if you are being valued by your employer to have to deal with this crap.

SOMETIMES THINGS JUST REALLY SUCK

For me, something crazy went down at 5:00 a.m. in front of four hundred starving and severely pissed-off factory workers in a ball-bearing plant in Nebraska. Yep. That happened. This was a major *What the hell am I doing here?* moment. When I was working at Healthways, I led a division of the company that provided a healthcare service called "biometric screening." A biometric screening is like a mini physical exam that is done on-site at a company location. In this case, a company paid us to come out and do the mini physical, which consisted of measuring body mass index and body fat, taking blood pressure readings, and doing a blood draw. Now, blood can be drawn from the human body in two ways. The first way is a simple finger prick, which is almost impossible to screw up, is essentially painless, and is not at all scary. The other way is called venipuncture, which is accomplished by sticking a needle into a vein in the arm and slowly extracting blood. This method is painful, scary, and ripe with ability to screw up. Even the name is terrible: vein-i-puncture. It sounds as if something awful is going to happen to your vein and then it is going to explode. The problem is, you cannot get a nicotine result from a finger stick, and because our customers wanted to know how many of their employees smoked, we used the much more challenging method of venipuncture.

The results of the biometric screening were to be reviewed not only by the company who hired us but were to be given to each employee as well so individuals could take action on any healthcare issues that came back. There were lots of potential problems with this business model, and we initially screwed up everywhere. Because we had to do these biometric screenings in random places across the country with only about thirty days of preparation time, we were not able to use our own staff and so had to outsource the work to independently contracted phlebotomists (people who draw blood for a living). Because these phlebotomists didn't work for us directly and didn't even work permanently for the company we used to find them, they had no real allegiance to us or to anyone. Some of these phlebotomists were terrific and were absolute professionals. Some of the phlebotomists were marginal at best in their attendance and job performance.

Back to my ball-bearing story. (Yes, ball bearings.) Did I mention the wind chill was negative twenty degrees when I left my hotel room in the middle of Nebraska at 4:00 in the morning? The streets were covered with several inches of ice, and my two-wheel-drive rental car went spinning all over the road as I headed to the manufacturing plant to oversee a biometric screening for about four hundred employees of the plant. I pulled into the parking lot of the giant, looming building in the dark, and no one seemed to be anywhere. The building seemed to extend for several blocks in each direction in the dark. I couldn't even find a door. After circling the building several times, bracing myself against the wind and cold, I finally found an entrance. Inside I walked around alone in parts of the plant where I probably wasn't supposed to be until I found the company's human resources manager, who nervously asked if everything was ready to go. She was nervous because here is the other obstacle to the venipuncture blood-draw method: to get an accurate result, the participants have to fast for at least eight hours. This means there were four hundred blue-collar, ball-bearing-making, tough men and women who were hungry as crap and waiting to get to work. I was about to be the guy who was responsible for sticking a sharp object in all of their arms so their employer could tell them to stop smoking. Additionally, the plant had shut down all of their manufacturing machines to do this screening event, so they were losing money by the minute.

"Are the phlebotomists with you?" the HR manager anxiously asked me.

The blood drained out of my face as I registered her question. It was now 5:00 a.m., and the phlebotomists were supposed to be there at 4:30 a.m. "You mean they aren't here yet?" I said.

The very painful answer to this question was "no." The phlebotomists pulled a no-show. They didn't answer the phone when I called them probably a thousand times from the corner of the plant while four hundred sets of glaring eyes watched my every move. The human resources manager was so pissed at me. I mean really pissed. The four hundred employees who had been fasting for eight hours were pissed at me. The CEO of the company was pissed at me. My boss was pissed at me. Everyone was pissed at me. What thought do you think went through my head?

> *What am I doing here? What the fuck am I doing here? I am standing in a ball-bearing plant in the middle of freezing Nebraska at 5:00 a.m. alone in front of four hundred angry blue-collar workers. Why am I here?! What the hell am I doing here?! Where the fuck is everyone else? Is this what senior directors of operations do? Is this what business school graduates do? Have ANY of my friends ever been in this shitty of a situation? What the fuck am I doing here?!*

Yes, guilty: I had a big old mental fit. I wanted to sink through the floor or turn and walk out the door and get on a plane and go home and apply for a job at Smoothie King. It sucked. It was a total *What the hell am I doing here?* moment. I felt like a failure. I felt like I was alone. I felt like I could not succeed in the role and nothing would go well and fixing this crap at its core was going to be impossible.

I have had dozens of these moments in my career. The highlight reel of my *What the hell am I doing here?* moments includes witnessing a mobster try to collect a debt in a dump of a hotel one night in New Jersey . . . spending Thanksgiving Day drinking Budweiser with coworkers at a Hooters after work . . . sprinting to make and miss hundreds of flights . . . and literally hundreds and hundreds of lonely dinners at the bars of mediocre hotel restaurants. There is a specific look on the face of a road warrior eating a lonely dinner at a hotel restaurant bar. We don't eat at a table, as the only thing lonelier than the hotel bar is a half-empty hotel-restaurant table. There we sit, scrolling through our phones, hearing a baseball game on the TV behind the bar but not watching it, and not even texting with our wives and husbands, as there just isn't anything to say.

> **Something I have learned:** Don't judge your entire job when you have "What the hell am I doing here?" moments.

THIS *IS* YOUR JOB

These experiences are going to happen, especially if you are putting yourself out there. In fact, you should expect some suffering in your career. You are going to be standing in your own ball-bearing plant one day wondering what the hell is going on. If you never have these moments, then you probably aren't pushing your career. And here is the deal: this *is* what senior directors of operations occasionally have to do. If they are in charge of the biometric-screening event operations and the shit hits the fan, *they* get on a plane in the freezing-ass cold and fly to Nebraska to make things right. *They* answer to the pissed-off CEO. *They* figure out how to minimize the chance of the screw-up happening again. If you want the reward of the larger responsibility, don't complain about the occasional pain of the larger responsibility. So when you find yourself in one of these moments, give yourself some emotional space and ask yourself a series of questions:

> ➤ Does this happen every week?
> ➤ Can I try to change or fix something that is broken to reduce the chance of this situation happening again?
> ➤ Is the rest of my job pretty good?

If the answers are no, yes, yes, then acknowledge your feelings, let them happen, and give yourself some time for the crappy day to pass. You have a normal job that has some things that are a pain in the ass, but generally things are okay. Welcome to your life.

If your answers are yes, no, no, then you have a shitty job. However, you may need that shitty job to pay your bills or help you advance your career and move you deeper into the Funnel. Usually when you have these feelings you are actually paying your dues. Dues are mainly paid early in your career but also can pop up later. An important point of dues, though, is that they actually make us better at our jobs, and they can be incredibly useful later in our careers. What did I learn from the ball-bearing incident? If I don't want to get yelled at by four hundred angry factory workers, build a better mousetrap. Make the business run better. Roll up my sleeves and put a process in place. Call the vendor and tell them to get their ass to my office so we can figure out how to never have phlebotomists miss another screening. Figure out a performance-based compensation model for the vendor that has penalties and bonuses for execution. And on and on and on.

Some of the pain points of paying your dues are in your control. For those instances, go to work on them. For the phlebotomist situation, I ended up spending about a year building an entirely new operating model for our wellness-screening business. Our team had to find a new vendor to build a new way of doing everything related to these screening events, from staffing to the shipping of the weighing scales and everything in between. It was a ton of work, but that is what I was hired to do! After a year of trying things, failing, tweaking, failing a little less, tweaking again, and then starting to have consistent success, we developed a really impressive operating structure to support the screening events. In my last year in that role, we screened over one hundred thousand people across thirty-two states in something like three hundred unique towns with a 99 percent positive rating from the participants. It was very rewarding to help move us to the point of a sustainable, successful operation.

WHAT CAN YOU LEARN?

If your situation is different and paying your dues is more systemic and you actually have a job that sucks most of the time, look up from your job and try to see what else you can learn. My neighbor's son worked one summer in college cleaning pots in the kitchen at a lodge out west. This was one of those summer experiences that are probably dying as students these days seek more focused work than washing dishes. I had several of these summers myself, and they were glorious. Probably the best was a summer in Jackson Hole, Wyoming, where I was gainfully employed in the complex trade of delivering bags of ice to grocery stores and gas stations. Trust me, it is hard to dress that shit up on a résumé.

So my neighbor's son is cleaning pots in the kitchen of this lodge. Giant pots. Pots that have been used in an industrial kitchen to feed hundreds of hungry tourists. This is a job of paying your dues, if there ever was one. If you looked up "paying your dues" in Wikipedia, it may have a picture of this guy cleaning some big-ass pots. You can envision him standing there in front of a big sink, slightly hungover, with a spray nozzle and a scrub brush. His fingers are wrinkled from weeks of moisture. His feet hurt, and his socks are constantly wet. His back hurts from awkwardly holding these giant damn pots. He is miserable. So how do you look up from this job and see what else you can learn? Opportunity is all around him.

Assume the lodge has two hundred rooms and the average nightly rate is $300, and that they are at an 80 percent occupancy rate year-round. These assumptions mean the guy is working for a business that generates over $17 million in annual revenue. This is a big business. So, what does that mean for the kitchen? Assume on average two meals a day are served out of the kitchen at an average price of $15 for two guests. This means the kitchen is generating $3.5 million in annual revenue for the lodge. The kitchen is also a decent-sized business. So, what does this mean for the guy? How can he turn his job cleaning pots into something that helps him build skills and get out of his current job?

It's easy really: just ask. Yes, ask. After his shift is over one day, he can go to the food and beverage manager and ask when a convenient time would be to talk to her for a few minutes. Whenever the guy gets the chance, he can explain that he has an interest in the hotel or professional services industry and would really like to learn more about how things work more broadly. He can ask if the manager would be willing to spend thirty minutes with him one afternoon when his shift is over explaining how the food and beverage part of the lodge works in more detail. Here are all of the aspects the guy eventually could learn by following this path:

> Vendor management: Who does the lodge use as a food supplier? Why did they choose these companies? How is the contract structured? How do they get paid? How do they ensure the vendor does a good job?
> Negotiation: How do the lodge and food vendors agree on the price? How often do they negotiate the price?
> Logistics: How do they get the food into the lodge? How do they manage the expiration dates of the food? How do they plan for the number of dinners for different days of the week?
> Recruiting and interviewing staff: How do they find staff? What questions do they ask in interviews?
> Payroll: How do they know how much to pay the employees? When do employees get raises and why?
> Staffing and scheduling: How do they know how many staff to hire?
> Management and leadership: How do they ensure the employees do a good job?
> Finance and managing a budget: How do they know if they are making money?

Every one of these categories could be learned by the guy by asking questions and building a relationship with the manager. If they cover all these questions, he can move on to the cleaning service, the gift shop, the website, and sales and marketing. There is literally almost every aspect of business occurring all around the lodge, including finance, sales and marketing, technology, operations, and human resources.

Most managers can appreciate someone wanting to learn the business. Most managers like to explain how things work. Most managers embrace this interest and curiosity. So the dues are paid at the kitchen sink, but at the end of three months, the guy could leave with a strong understanding of how core business departments and functions work. This knowledge is highly transferrable from the hotel and hospitality industry to many other industries. He could leave with relationships with managers and potentially owners of the lodge. He might discover the hotel industry is not for him, but he is intrigued by sales and marketing. Perhaps he goes back the following summer and does an internship with the hotel's sales and marketing department and builds a foundation for a career in that industry. One day many years later he may be the creative director of a New York advertising agency, and it all started in front of some dirty pots in the kitchen and a casual thirty-minute conversation many years earlier.

I can feel you rolling your eyes at this entire story. People, this is how it happens! This is exactly how careers unfold! Careers are random and messy and scrappy. Careers don't unfold by accident, though. Pay your dues. Look up. Ask questions. Be curious. Build relationships. And all of this may begin from a moment of saying to yourself, *What the hell am I doing here?* So, who are you talking to today? What are you learning new today?

> *Something I have learned:* Most of you will have to pay your dues. You should expect this in your career. Most of these moments will help you grow and develop.

GIVE YOURSELF SPACE (AGAIN)

You can find ways to improve a business process through these moments. You can learn how to manage clients effectively through these moments. You can develop humility in these moments. You can practice perseverance in these moments. You cannot just run away, though. If you simply bail out when you have these moments, you are taking away from your own learning. Suffering is part of life. Suffering should be expected. Those who have found the most peace learn to embrace suffering and know that it not only is to be expected, but suffering is also where you grow the most. Give yourself the space to see these moments for what they are and observe yourself in the situation versus reacting to the situation. What does creating this space look like in practice? Observing yourself in a shitty situation looks like you saying this in your head:

Well, this sucks. This is a really shitty situation. This is a pain in the ass and is going to be a pain in the ass, but I probably will take something away from this and I know this moment will not last forever. I just need to endure this situation and get through it the best I can, and then look for the growth areas on the back end.

If you can find this type of space, you can come out of these instances not only okay but having grown from the experience.

9

I DON'T KNOW HOW TO MANAGE MY BOSS

The boss issue comes up often. Some bosses are highly engaged to the point of micromanaging, while others are hands-off and difficult to read. Most bosses are somewhere in the middle. Occasionally, though, you may end up with a boss who is an ass. I have actually only had one boss who was a real ass. It was very early in my career, and it was short-lived, as she was shown the door by the company soon after her promotion to manager. Beyond that experience, the closest I have come to having a challenging boss is having a lot of bosses in a relatively short period of time. I'm talking five different bosses in two and a half years, which has happened twice. Every six months I would get a new boss, who would try to come in and tell me all the areas of my job that he thought could work more effectively without really understanding the departmental function or market environment. Having this carousel of managers was frustrating at times but enlightening overall, as it yielded some valuable tactics and understanding of human behaviors. When it comes to bosses, there are all types: the benevolent dictator, the passive-aggressive, the straight shooter, the buddy/buddy, the clueless, the oddball, and yes, the full-on ass. When I reference the ass-boss, I am putting aside anything illegal and/or against company policy, including sexual harassment and verbal abuse. I am not qualified to provide any context for those situations.

THE ASS-BOSS

This AB (ass-boss) is just an ass. You will typically know if your boss is an ass. You just will.

> **Something I have learned:** If you are the only one who thinks your boss is an ass, then it may actually be you who can't handle the job you are doing. If several others also feel your boss is an ass, he or she is likely an ass.

There is not much worse professionally than having to wake up in the morning and immediately dread going to your job if your boss is an ass. The feeling of dread just hovers over you. The primary difficulty in having an ass-boss is the lack of control. It doesn't feel like you can change the environment, and it feels like your ass-boss owns your every move. If his flaw is micromanagement, you know when it is coming and you know what it looks like. His probing questions make your skin crawl and you can't escape it. If his flaw is self-protection, you know that as soon as a problem arises, the blame is about to get punted by your ass-boss down to you or others. You end up taking the fall for something he has done. These managers suck.

It amazes me that there are still shitty bosses out there. In a world with so much transparency and communication, it just amazes me that a boss who is an ass can still maintain a leadership position. There are many different ways a manager can do a poor job of leading people, but it's important to note that *a bad boss is not one who requires you to do the job that you signed up for*. A demanding boss is not necessarily a bad boss, and a bad boss is not necessarily demanding.

Your goal with an AB is either to outlast him until he gets fired for being an ass or to insulate yourself from his ass-ness. It is important that you recognize an AB and acknowledge the feelings you are going to have working for him. Additionally, it will be important for you to have some practical tactics and methods for dealing with one. In fact, knowing how to manage any kind of boss is a critical skill to success and sanity.

> **Something I have learned:** *The tactics are generally the same for managing any kind of boss, no matter the kind of boss she or he is.*

These tactics are reasonably universal in helping you manage your boss:

1. Know what is expected of you.

2. Keep your manager updated on your work.
3. Seek help and assistance.
4. No surprises ever.

KNOW WHAT IS EXPECTED OF YOU

It is difficult to do a good job unless you know what is expected of you and how you will be measured. When you are hired into a position, you may be given a job description that explains what you are supposed to do. Job descriptions usually detail the activities that a job entails, not the actual results or outcomes the job is supposed to deliver. For you to have a chance at meeting your manager's expectations of you, you need to understand both the required activities and the desired outcomes you are responsible for delivering.

When I was leading the wellness business at Healthways, my team was responsible for scheduling, preparing for, and operating biometric screenings. To accomplish these activities, we had many subactivities, and then more activities within those subactivities. There were literally hundreds of activities that were required to schedule, plan, and execute one of our wellness screenings. These activities were part of our job functions. However, the *outcome* that we were responsible for was the satisfaction of our clients based on the employee experience as well as the delivery of an individual wellness report to those participating employees. My manager did not only measure my performance on the activities, he measured whether our clients were happy and if the individuals received their reports. Similarly, when I was a buyer at Dollar General, my activities were to meet with suppliers, review products, manage orders, and plan inventory. However, the outcomes or results I was responsible for were sales and profit of our products each month and year.

Knowing the results or outcomes you are responsible for helps inform your activities. If you don't know the outcomes you are responsible for in your job, then you need to ask your manager. This may seem like a basic task, but don't be surprised if you have jobs along the way where this part of your job is not made clear to you. The conversation with your manager doesn't have to be complex and can look something like:

> "I have a solid understanding of the activities you want me to do for my role. I want to make sure, though, that I am thinking about those activities in a broader context of the results or outcomes you want me to accomplish on a monthly or yearly basis. I would enjoy catching up with you to get your thoughts, so I can ensure I am aligned to your expectations."

MANAGE YOUR MANAGER

A second tactic that is helpful is to keep your manager updated on your work, so she almost never has to ask you for a status update on something. Nothing gives a manager anxiety more than uncertainty or a feeling of disconnection with the critical activities of the business. If you don't have set one-on-one meetings with your manager, gently suggest you could benefit from her expertise on your initiatives. Your manager may not ever ask for a detailed update, so you can just create one and start sending it to her with an explanation of what you are sending and why.

Here's an example of what you could say:

> "Donna, I am sending you this update as a way to keep you informed of the important initiatives I am

working on currently. This may help you stay connected to the work items you have assigned to me as well. You will notice there is a column for me to emphasize where I may need your input on a specific initiative. Perhaps we can use this as a framework for when we catch up regularly. Let me know how this works for you and if you have any suggestions. Thanks much!"

Use a consistent update methodology in those one-on-one sessions so she can quickly understand the status of your work. There are lots of different tools and ways to do this, either through basic ways, such as Excel or Word, or more sophisticated applications, such as Salesforce, Asana, TrackVia, or Basecamp. Below is an Excel template I have used frequently and that is a helpful way to organize updates on your nonrecurring work.

Category	Desired Q1 Outcome	Estimated % of Time	Status	Needed to make Green	Support needed from you
		25%			
		25%			
Talent	< Fully staffed across all open positions. <Annual goals established for each employee	15%	< 65% staffed for open positions with pipeline of candidates for nurse positions very light < First draft of goals for all positions complete. Target completion by November 1st	< Need to activate contract staffing company by Octobver 15th to be fully staffed by December 1st	< Approval to use the same contracting company as last year < Review draft of goals and provide input by Oct 15th
		25%			
	Total	100%			

The "Category" is the type of work you are doing and will be unique to your job and your company. The "Desired Outcome" for that time period is what you want to have completed by a specific time. In this example, it is a quarterly time period. The next column is an estimated percentage of the time you are spending on the category. The percentages will shift and change on a regular basis as the priorities of your job change and shift throughout the year. The color coding in this column of red, yellow, green is your way of alerting your manager to any problem areas. Green represents "on track" for achieving the outcome in the defined time period. Yellow represents potential risk of not achieving the outcome. Red means high risk of not achieving the outcome. You should be honest with your manager about the risks, as I am always skeptical of an employee who always has everything green. In fact, having all green usually means something is not listed on the tracking file. The "Status" is a quick summary of the recent work or activities completed or any objective data on the desired outcome. The column "Needed to Make Green" is a place for you to tell your manager what you think needs to happen to get the category back on track if it is yellow or red. This column is your chance to try to solve the problem and let your manager react to your suggestion. The last column of "Support Needed from You" is to note the activities or decisions you need from your manager to move the initiative along to completion. Note that you should give your manager due dates for the items you need her to complete.

If you have more of a recurring-work role, you can share any performance metrics on your recurring work. Also, if you run a larger team that has ongoing performance metrics, you can include those metrics in some sort of dashboard. Most managers will already be asking you about these types of metrics, though, and will already have some forum to discuss them.

SEEK HELP AND ASSISTANCE

The third tactic to managing your boss is to seek help and assistance. Managers expect their employees to be reasonably self-sufficient, yet they do not expect their employees to be perfect. It is perfectly acceptable for you to go to your manager for input, suggestions, and help when you have a question or an obstacle. However, when you seek assistance, always have a potential answer to your question or suggestion for your problem. Having a potential answer or suggestion will help show that you have thought about solving the problem yourself and have taken the time to consider a solution. You can explain the problem and your potential solution to your manager and ask for his perspective. Don't try to do everything on your own. Typically, managers are managers because they have skills and knowledge that their staff does not. It will be beneficial to use those skills and that knowledge to help you overcome obstacles.

NO SURPRISES EVER

The last principle is no surprises, ever. You should keep your manager informed of any failures or potential failures. You can help her help you by letting her know if something isn't working well.

> **Something I have learned:** Don't try to slip a failure or potential failure by your manager.

If you try to slip something by your manager and she discovers the failure, you will have lost some portion of her trust in both your honesty and your competency. You will be much better served to actively alert your manager of these situations. Just own the failure openly and candidly. As before, you will want to bring potential solutions to the problem when you notify her. Your actions may not be perfect, but it will show your manager that you have the ability to stay grounded as you work to solve the problem. And by assuring her that you will keep her informed even when the wheels are coming off, you will build trust with your manager that will serve you in the future. I have had many, many failures in my career both large and small (though most failures tend to feel large when they are actually happening). It is likely that you won't remember most of them if you are able to address them as quickly and effectively as possible.

These four tactics won't cover all the unique situations you will encounter with different types of managers, but they will give you a good framework to know how to navigate interactions with your boss so that you can support one another effectively even in the worst disaster moments.

Managing your boss requires managing yourself. And there is no substitute for knowing your business, your priorities, and your plan.

Early in my career, I viewed the concept of "managing up" as an exercise in relationship building—be accessible, dependable, and supportive. Get the job done and done well, on time. What I've learned over the course of my career is that you can get by this way and enjoy a productive relationship with your manager when you are in a position of needing to deliver on directed work—specific, detailed assignments, often one or two at a time in successive order. Check the box and move on to the next.

However, as you advance in your career, you begin to take on responsibility for more self-directed work, where you are working within a set of broad objectives and rough timelines. Here, you must determine the specific assignments for you and/or your team, establish the priorities, and deliver against a set of broad expectations. To manage your boss now, you need first to organize and manage yourself.

Start first with expectations and work backward. What is the result we're after and/or your manager's vision for the end product? What are the hard constraints (timing, sign-off, budget limits)?

Here's where you need to build an open relationship with your manager and take the time to learn about how they set and view the expectations they communicate to you. Are they more literal or speak figuratively? What do they most value (attention to detail, not being surprised)? This is a process that you continue throughout your work together.

Once you understand the explicit and implicit expectations, you must plan. The concept of a "One Place" to capture my projects and tasks has always been with me, from the days of my first Franklin Planner. But having the place to write down your to-dos is only part of the battle. It has been enormously helpful for me to add the concept of a personal dashboard to support my recurring one-on-one conversations with my manager. It's forced me to not just jot down my tasks, but to spend time each week organizing them and, most importantly, checking where I'm spending time relative to the results that are expected.

The dashboard also allows me to drive the conversation with my manager versus react to questions or concerns about any one project. A critically important component of the dashboard is the "Support Needed from You" column, where I can be explicit about the barriers I'm facing in the work, the actions that need to be taken, and the support that is needed. I remember a manager early in my career telling me to "come with solutions and not with problems," and this feels like a manifestation of that—driving the conversation with my manager to what is needed to solve the problem or advance the work.

The other valuable learning for me has been to be able to keep my focus—and the focus of my conversations with my manager— on the results and not the activities. It's an easy trap to talk about all the stuff that has been done, or that needs to be done. But the work started with an expectation, and the conversations along the work started with an expectation, and the conversations along the way need to stay grounded in that to ensure that all that activity is advancing you to the result.

The importance of these principles and planning only increasewhen you are yourself managing a team who wants to know they too are focused on the most important work, that you are helping them demonstrate that they know their business well, and that they are having an impact. And you can only deliver on that if you are, first and foremost, managing yourself.

—Eric F., Vice President of Operations

DEEP IN THE FUNNEL:
FEELINGS AND EXPERIENCES ADVANCED IN YOUR CAREER

10
I FEEL LIKE I WANT TO BE THE MANAGER

A re you sure about that? A lot of you may get to this point in your career and think you want to manage other people. Often people think the only path of promotion is to go from being a doer to being a manager. This progression is normal for most functions or departments in that you start as a doer, then progress to a manger of doers, then progress to a manager of managers, and so on. However, not every job or career develops this way. For example, a chief strategy officer may only have a few people who work for him, versus a chief operating officer, who may have hundreds or thousands of people who work for her, yet both are senior positions. Before you rush off to apply for the manager position, it is important to understand the role of the manager.

THE JOB OF THE MANAGER

The manager is responsible for the collective performance of the team or group. A manager typically has specific goals she has to achieve for the month, quarter, and year. These goals can be operational and financial. When I led my first team at Dollar General, our main goals were on-time deliveries of merchandise and overall shipping costs per box. These two main goals were a culmination of a lot of smaller tasks that a group of six people did on a daily basis. If my team did these small tasks well on a routine basis, our trucks showed up on time and were as full as we could get them, and our goals were achieved. My boss and my boss's boss looked at these metrics every month. If we were at or above our goal for these two metrics, life was good. If we were below the goal for these metrics, I had better know why we were below our goals and I also better have had a plan to get us back on track. Being a manager of people often means you are responsible for a broad scope of goals.

> *Something I have learned:* When you are the manager, your job is to deal with everything that gets in the way of your team's ability to achieve its goals.

What gets in the way of team goals? Two things get in the way of team goals: interesting challenges and people stuff. All kinds of interesting challenges and all kinds of people stuff get in the way. And as the manager, you get to work on the interesting challenges.

However, you also have to deal with the people stuff. Some of the people stuff is normal people stuff, and some of the people stuff is crap.

THE FUN STUFF VERSUS THE CRAP STUFF

The fun stuff to work on is the interesting challenges. You will spend a lot of time solving business problems to make your team work better, faster, less expensively, more efficiently, more effectively, or whatever it is that your team does. These challenges are never complete, as businesses are complex and ever-changing organizations in complex and ever-changing industries. Solving these problems is usually interesting and exciting. You will see the best in your people come out and you will be proud of individuals and teams for the great work they do to help you solve these problems.

The crap stuff, though, is another story. As the manager, you deal with all the crap. Most of the crap is people crap. People crap includes disagreements, manipulation, turf wars, drama, home problems, family problems, personal problems, and everything else that comes with those areas. Every manager has to deal with this stuff. Sometimes you have no crap and sometimes you are bombarded with crap. I have dealt with all kinds, and it can be exhausting.

I once had an employee in our department who worked in a small customer-support call center and was paid hourly, so she clocked in and out of a time-keeping system. In looking at her time in our payroll-approval system, I noticed her work hours were considerably longer than the other call-center staff. (Hourly employees are eligible for overtime pay, which is expensive and so it is normally monitored closely.) Through the payroll system, I was able to determine that her start time was earlier than the rest of the employees almost every day. Here is the catch, though. I have always liked to get to the office early, and this employee was logging a start time that was around the same time I typically arrived for work. The call-center employees sat near my office, so I questioned the validity of her clock-in time, as I had not remembered seeing her in the mornings. To validate the clock-in time, I asked our building services to check the time logs on the electronic door locks, which record the arrival of each employee via a scan of his/her electronic badge. After pulling this information together, I discovered the employee logged her clock-in time at about 7:15 a.m. every day, but the door logs showed the employee arrived at about 7:45 a.m. almost every day. It became apparent that the employee was arriving at 7:45 a.m. and then putting 7:15 a.m. as her start time. Well, this is stealing. This is stealing 30 minutes of paid time every day. Employees often see a company as an amorphous entity that has unlimited funds and is not associated with an actual person. The reality is that this employee was stealing 30 minutes every day x 240 workdays per year x $12 per hour = $1,440. Our company had about three thousand employees, so if every employee snuck an extra $1,440 worth of time they didn't work, it would total over $4.3 million in additional payroll for unworked time. This amount of money can be the difference in a company existing profitably or tanking.

Guess who gets to confront the employee and ask her about the time discrepancy? As the manager, you do! Remember when I mentioned the crap? This is the crap. When I sat down with this employee and showed her the clock-in time versus the door badge time that had occurred for several weeks, she denied it was true. When I asked her if she could explain how day after day, her door badge showed her arriving thirty minutes after she started work, she just said she didn't know.

Huh?

Insanity.

So, I then had to do a formal write-up, documenting the situation, giving her a written warning, notifying human resources, and conducting a meeting with all employees to remind them of the clock-in policy. The next day, miraculously, her clock-in time started occurring after the door badge time.

Literally the next day.

Insanity.

As the manager of this employee, I spent at least ten hours working on this situation, and it contributed absolutely nothing to the value we brought to our customers.

The normal-people stuff can be equally as time consuming, but it also needs your attention. These are things like employee illness, family deaths, problems with children, and other things that just happen to all of us. It is your job to continue to run the group or department or business when these situations occur in the lives of your employees. However, it is also your job to support your employees with compassion during these times. I learned this lesson early in my career, and I will never forget it. If you have ever taken a Myers-Briggs personality test, you know that it tells you your personality tendencies. Mine is typically either an ENTJ or an ESTJ. Either way, I do not have a strong "Feeling" component. This basically means that the human aspect of a decision or situation is not my primary focus. At this point in my career, I am very much aware of this tendency and work to overcome it, but it is my "base layer." Early in my career, I had not developed the self-awareness or the strategies to compensate for my base layer, and I often overlooked the human element of situations. I will never forget learning the hard way the importance of compassion. At that time, my team consisted of a group of employees, all of whom worked remotely and all of whom moved around from place to place, and so I only met with them in person about once a month. A member of my team had lost her father a few weeks before we had our regularly scheduled in-person meeting. When we sat down to meet, we jumped straight into business concerns, discussing performance metrics, challenges, and important initiatives to improve our operation. She was a great employee and operator, and it was, as usual, a productive meeting. However, when we finished, she asked if she could give me some risk-free feedback. She said I was a great manager at all the operational activities and I could inspire and lead people well. She then said, "My father died three weeks ago, and you never called me and you didn't ask me today how I was doing."

Ouch.

Shit.

What the hell kind of person am I?

She then explained she was not telling me this because she was mad at me. Rather, she was sharing this because she cared about me. She knew this was a gap in my leadership, and she wanted to share her observation with me so I could become a better leader throughout my entire career. She asked if she could give me some advice on leadership. She said, "You need to soften up." She went on to explain that she did not mean I needed to go easy on the team regarding tasks and objectives, but rather I needed to soften up as a human being. I needed to see the human element of situations. Her observation and advice hit me like a dump truck. I immediately took out a piece of paper from my notebook and wrote the words "Soften up!" on it. I keep a notebook of articles and different papers that have helped me along the way, and this piece of paper is laminated in that notebook.

I had several takeaways from that experience. One is that I try to surround myself with people who have a stronger feeling component to their tendencies. Another is that I have tried to train myself to give a situation the space to see the human element.

> *Something I have learned:* As the boss or the manager, your job is to see the human element of the situations and decisions that affect your employees and to address those aspects as well.

As for the tactical elements of the manager's role, all managers generally have the same five responsibilities: hire good people, set the strategy, monitor the behaviors, measure the results, and model the culture. The size and scale of these aspects will vary between the first-line manager and the CEO, but these are the core aspects of any manager's job. Within each of these five aspects are dozens of subactivities that make each one of these work effectively.

HIRING GOOD PEOPLE

Hiring good people is really difficult to do. It is not difficult because there aren't good people available to be hired, but rather because hiring is not something we do regularly and therefore we are not good at doing it. Your day-to-day jobs are to lead a sales team or a design team or a finance team or whatever team, and you know all about how those functions work. You have experience in sales, design, finance, or whatever it is that you do because you have done that stuff all day for years. What you have not done is hire people all day for years. In fact, you have only spent a very small part of your job hiring people, and therefore you are probably not very good at it. This competency gap is totally normal, as most people are not good at hiring new employees. I am still not very good at hiring people. I always end up getting so excited to talk to someone about the different aspects of the healthcare business and to learn more about her perspectives on things that I end up just shooting the shit during the interview. I also just believe in most people's abilities and probably give them too much of the benefit of the doubt.

Because I know that I am generally not very good at hiring people, even after having hired dozens and dozens of employees, I surround myself with others who are good at hiring, and I also use a specific methodology. I used to work with someone who was terrific at hiring people. He could spot areas of experience or skill and could hone in on those areas with the perfect probing and direct question. He would let awkwardness sit in an interview no matter how uncomfortable it became. He and I were hiring people at Dollar General for a position that required a lot of analytical thinking, autonomy, and problem solving, and we needed an objective way of filtering the candidates. We decided that in the middle of the interview we would randomly stop the interview and give the candidate a calculator, a piece of paper, and a pen, and we would tell the candidate we wanted them to calculate and tell us the total weight of all of the ice in a professional hockey rink. We then would leave the room for about five minutes to give them the space to figure out the answer. We were not the first people to use this tactic, as most of the management consulting and finance firms have used these tactics for years; however, I am fairly certain we were the first discount retailing company to use the method.

The range of answers we received was wide and hysterical. The best candidates made a series of rational assumptions, such as the surface area of the rink, the depth of the ice, the weight of a one-foot-by-one-foot block of the ice, etc. This group would have a bunch of calculations written out on the paper to explain their answer to us. They understood that we were asking the question to test their problem-solving skills and would have a mathematical answer to present to us. At the other end of the spectrum were the people who totally froze up (no pun intended), and there was nothing on the paper, the pen and calculator had not moved, and their faces were a few shades paler than when we left the room. This group was clearly not wired for this type of problem solving. The middle group was somewhere in between. You don't have to use this tactic to hire good people, but there is a lesson in here.

> **Something I have learned:** *Have a specific structure to the way you hire people.*

A good practice is to have a set of the same questions to ask every candidate who is applying for the position. Think about questions that are relevant to the work you need the person to do. Additionally, think back to chapter 2 on the need for preparation. Three questions you should ask every candidate you interview:

1. "Tell me everything you did to prepare for this interview today."
2. "Tell me everything you know about our company."
3. "Tell me everything you know about me."

If a candidate cannot answer all three of these questions quickly and with detail, I never hire them. I actually start almost every interview with these three questions, and if someone fails to answer these three well, unless their experience blows me away enough to warrant continuing, I sometimes end the interview right then. If a candidate does not have the intelligence to know that he needs to prepare for the interview, then I don't want him working on my team.

Beyond these three questions, it is helpful to have other questions that relate to the position, your industry, how they would handle a certain situation, or something that allows you to see their skills or experience. Keeping a spreadsheet or notes with a ranking of one through five with comments on how they answered the questions will allow you to go back after the interview and compare candidates more objectively.

Lastly, as a tactic for hiring good people, strive really hard to have a diverse pool of applicants. If you are a white dude in your midthirties and everyone else on your team is a white dude in his midthirties, you are missing out on representation of a lot of the rest of the world. Setting goals for diversity in the pool of applicants for an open job is a great way to see how diversity can help your team perform better. You will find that diversity can improve performance.

SETTING THE STRATEGY

If you are the CEO, setting the strategy is a big deal, with significant long-term implications for the company. Setting the strategy for a small team is also important, but different. The strategy for a small team could be a list of the main initiatives you want to accomplish together as a team over the course of an entire year. These could be things such as getting twenty new customers, improving customer satisfaction to 90-plus percent, launching a new product, or anything that is within your team's control. Setting a strategy is valuable because it gives your team a shared objective and a contextual framework for the specific tasks assigned them. Setting a strategy is also valuable because it forces you as the boss to actually think about what the strategy is going to be! I recommend having a working session with your team to discuss the strategy together. It is important for the team to feel connected to the development of key work areas. The list of strategic items for the year should not be long, perhaps four to six in total. Once you have the strategy, you should talk about it all the time. I mean be a freaking broken record of these strategic goals. Tie back your requests and tasks and meetings to these strategic items. Everyone on your team should know them and be able to reference them. Without your verbal momentum, though, they will drift away, and the team will lose that broader context and common cause.

MONITORING THE BEHAVIORS

Monitoring the behaviors is probably the most difficult of the five main manager areas. Many managers end up in one ditch or another and either micromanage people or are disconnected from the important tasks and initiatives that support the strategy. Finding a balance is essential. Doing so empowers your team to work on the tasks you have assigned them and to feel you support them without driving them crazy.

> **Something I have learned:** Your job as the manager is not to do all the work your employees do.

There may be times when you are a player-coach and you are the manager and also do some of the same work as your employees. However, most of the time when you are a manager, you are doing a different type of work than your direct reports. This means you have to delegate. Delegation is one of the most essential parts of being a manager, but it is often uncomfortable for managers for all kinds of reasons. Some managers are people-pleasers and delegating feels mean. Others struggle with delegating, as they think their employees don't have the capacity for more work. Regardless, one of your jobs is to get the most productivity out of your employees without burning them out. There are some very specific and effective tactics to delegation: context, vision, deadlines, prioritizing, and updating.

Almost no one likes to do work that they don't know *why* they are doing it. Nothing is as demeaning as being told to do something without any context of why you are being asked to do it. Providing employees with information about the larger context shows them you value and trust them. When you explain the "what" of an initiative or task, always include the context, or the "why." For example, "I want you to check the arrival of every shipment of the weight scales going to the biometric screenings." Why, though?! Explain the context and "the why."

> "If we can confirm the scales arrive at every biometric screening, we will never have to cancel a screening event for missing equipment. This performance in turn will increase our customer satisfaction, which will give us more referrals for potential new customers. If we have more referrals for potential new customers, we will be able to meet our sales targets for this year."

What could have appeared to be an incredibly boring activity for your employee now is connected to a much larger and important company goal. Notice how you can take context deeper into the company. I could have stopped with the first sentence about not having to cancel a screening event. What is the context around the importance of not cancelling a screening event, though? Take the context further. I could have stopped with the sentence of referrals, but kept taking it further. The longer the thread of the context, the more employees will understand the importance.

The second step is to give the vision for the work to be done. The vision helps bring to life what your expectation is of the end product. Without this vision, your employee may go work on something for a month and come back with something very different from what you had in mind. You need to paint the picture of the final result of their work as well as the general steps to get there.

> "I think the finished product of this work is to find an automated way for us to receive emails when the scales arrive at our screening events so you no longer have to check them. You will want to have a process defined with a shipping company and have done some sort of small, successful pilot in parallel to our normal process. You probably will want to talk to our fulfillment department to see if they have any existing shipping-company contacts we can use and then let the sales team know we are testing this as well. Also check with Mike in IT, as he will be able to help with an email interface."

Notice the explanation of your vision of the end product: having established a vendor relationship and having completed a small pilot of a process. This is the vision for the actual end of this body of work so the employee can now understand what his task is. You also gave him a general framework for the first few steps of the task so he can know where to begin.

The next step is to provide a deadline. One time I met with a first-time manager who was struggling to know how to delegate work to her employees. With frustration, she said she wanted one of her direct reports to step up and complete an initiative without her prompting. Through our conversation, we uncovered several missing tactics of her attempted delegation. She was frustrated over her employee's lack of progress against an initiative, yet she had not given the employee a specific deadline for the task. She felt that the employee should just work on the task with diligence and get it done. Without a deadline, though, the two people may have different perspectives on the urgency. Your employees cannot read your mind, so you need to be specific with the deadlines for the final product as well as deadlines for milestones.

> "You should try to have this finished by mid-May,
> which means you probably need to start the pilot by
> April 1."

When you provide a deadline, it will help if you ask the following question: "Do you think this deadline is reasonable to you?" You are not asking this to force your employee to say yes. If they say yes but know they can't deliver on the deadline, then the deadline is useless. Your purpose in asking this question is to generate some dialogue on prioritization.

Prioritization is often the next step in the process of delegation. If you ask your employee the deadline question and he either answers "no" or he answers "yes," but his body language is saying "oh shit," you probably need to conduct a prioritization session with him. The purpose of a prioritization session is to create time for your employee to work on this item or to determine that the item is actually not as important as something else. To do this prioritization, you can schedule a dedicated hour to sit down with your employee to go through his recurring and nonrecurring work in detail. Have him come to this session with a list of the initiatives he is working on and the order of priority that he feels is appropriate. You then can evaluate the initiatives he is working on together to consider holistically where to put this new initiative. Almost every time I do one of these prioritization sessions with an employee, I find a couple of items that can be moved down in priority, delegated to someone else, or stopped entirely. The beauty in doing this prioritization with your employee is that he feels supported by you and is involved in the process of prioritizing. Lastly, he will have vital context around why certain initiatives are prioritized.

The last step in delegation is to receive updates, which we touched on last chapter. Receiving updates is critical and is often done inefficiently or not at all.

> **Something I have learned:** It is not your job or responsibility to remember to ask for updates from your employees on their work.

If you have eight employees who work for you and each one has ten different initiatives, it is impossible for you to keep track of eighty unique initiatives. As a manager, your value is leading people and solving problems, not babysitting the updates of your employees. It is the responsibility of your employees to manage the updates to you on their own initiatives in a way that is predictable and consistent. You can create predictability by requesting that each of your employees sends you status updates on their initiatives with a set frequency, such as biweekly. A good reinforcement of this frequency is to establish a thirty- to sixty-minute one-on-one meeting to review the status updates. During these status-update sessions, your employees can ask you questions and you can provide input on any problem areas. Your employee should be the one to schedule the meeting, send you update information in advance, and lead the discussion. This meeting is *their* meeting to use you as a resource to help them complete their work. To generate consistency in these update sessions, they can use the same template you use with your manager referenced in the prior chapter.

Category	Desired Q1 Outcome	Estimated % of Time	Status	Needed to make Green	Support needed from you
		25%			
		25%			
Talent	< Fully staffed across all open positions. <Annual goals established for each employee	15%	< 65% staffed for open positions with pipeline of candidates for nurse positions very light < First draft of goals for all positions complete. Target completion by November 1st	< Need to activate contract staffing company by Octobver 15th to be fully staffed by December 1st	< Approval to use the same contracting company as last year < Review draft of goals and provide input by Oct 15th
		25%			
	Total	100%			

This type of template is very helpful for managing employees with a large amount of nonrecurring work, as this is the most difficult type of work to keep track of consistently. Your employees would maintain this type of document, update it biweekly, and send it to you before your catch-up meeting.

As their manager, you can help your staff stay organized by not bombarding them with random tasks or requests via email. I suggest you bundle those requests as you think of them and then delegate and discuss collectively with your staff in a one-on-one meeting. A critical part of this practice is for you to have an organized way to keep track of all the tasks you want to delegate in between one-on-one meetings. I suggest using your digital One Place for this. You can create a task under the category of "Talent" for each of your direct reports, named "Frazer 1:1," for example. Think about this task as your agenda for your next one-on-one that accumulates over time. Within this task, you add a subtask or comments on the items you want to cover in your next one-on-one. In that next one-on-one session, your employee brings her tracking document and you simply open your One Place and explain all of the items you want her to own. Obviously, this process does not work if an item you need to delegate is urgent. In that case, a phone call or email is necessary, but you can also add to your one-on-one One Place task to confirm she has added the urgent ones to her file.

Whatever method you choose, I suggest you make it consistent across all of your direct reports, so you will be familiar with how to consume the information and your interactions will therefore be more efficient. Imagine receiving this type of update on a biweekly basis from your staff. You would almost never have uncertainty about the status of their nonrecurring work. Additionally, your catch-up meetings will be incredibly efficient, as you will be able to focus quickly on a couple of important areas. One of the data points this type of framework gives you is the allocation of time your staff is spending on certain areas. For example, the document may show 10 percent on a part of the business that you feel is very important and 50 percent on an area that is much less important. Because you have this context from your staff, you can work with her to shift priorities from one area to another. Without this information, your staff may spend months working on parts of the business that are not the most important ones. The framework also will help you see any areas that are yellow or red, so you can quickly focus on solving the problem areas with your staff. Lastly, the column for actions needed from you tells you exactly what is needed on your end.

Now you can understand the complexity of monitoring the behaviors of your employees. Using a defined method for delegating and keeping up with all of the behaviors is essential to staying in the middle ground, where you are not micromanaging nor are you totally disconnected from the important work. If you provide context, describe the vision, establish a deadline, help prioritize, and receive status updates, your delegation model can work very effectively.

MEASURING THE RESULTS

Measuring the results should be the easiest part of your job once it is set up. With every team, there are sets of measurements or metrics that describe the performance of that team, i.e. how they are doing against their goals. These metrics may be financial, such as revenue per thing, cost per thing, profit per thing, or one of several other ways to measure financial performance. An example of a financial metric might be average revenue per customer at a coffee shop or average revenue per consultant at a consulting company. Metrics can be based on speed or efficiency, such as time required to do a task or maximum use of a resource. Some examples of these could be average speed to answer a call for a call center or click-through conversion rate for a web-based company. These types of measures are essential for a manager to know on a routine basis. I won't spend a lot of time on this topic, as again, most companies have these metrics established already.

Ultimately, you should accept a supervisor or manager position with humility. Being the boss does not give you the license to be an ass. You have been trusted by the company you work for to lead and develop other people, not treat them like dirt.

> *Something I have learned:* Your employees are not there to serve you, they are there to serve the needs of your company.

If you want to know if you are doing a good job as a manager, generally your employees should feel that they would hypothetically "purchase" expertise from you because you help them do their job more effectively. This doesn't mean everyone will be happy all the time. Again, you have to deal with the crap, and when you do, someone usually isn't happy. Happiness, however, is not the goal of a work team. Happiness can be a by-product or a result of having clear goals and expectations, having a positive culture, and doing work that is meaningful and interesting. The success of the company transcends everything, and if one of your employees ever gets to a place where he doesn't put the success of the company first, then something is out of alignment (which could include the company), and he should probably move on to something else.

MODELING THE CULTURE

Finally, as the boss, you need to live the culture of the company, assuming that your company has a positive culture. If your company does not have a positive culture, then you need to create a positive culture within your team. You can actually feel the difference in teams within the same company that have varying cultures. I cover team culture and principles in much more detail in chapter 11.

Being a manager can be very rewarding if you enjoy that role and these tactics and methods resonate with you. It has been incredibly fulfilling for me to see people who worked for me in the past develop and grow through their careers as managers. It has been even more fulfilling to see others adopt and spread these same tactics to their own teams. Be the manager for the correct reasons and understand the importance of your role.

11
I FEEL UNGROUNDED

The feeling of being ungrounded is difficult to describe but easy to recognize. This ungrounded feeling is like a haze of anxiety that seeps into your psyche. You feel that something is missing or behind schedule, but you can't identify what it is. Some of these ungrounded feelings stem from a lack of control or organization over your workload or your time, which we covered in depth in chapter 6. However, sometimes this feeling is on a higher plane. You can have all the tactical workload and time management pieces in place and functioning well, but you just feel you are missing something from a leadership standpoint. To address these feelings, you need to understand how you think about your work.

YOUR GLOBAL FRAMEWORK

Very few managers consider what their job is at the highest level. As we covered in the last chapter, most managers operate within the following five requirements of their job:

1. Hire and support good people.
2. Set the strategy.
3. Monitor the behaviors.
4. Measure the results.
5. Model the culture.

I call these five elements the Global Framework. The Global Framework is the highest level of thinking, as it what you are supposed to do for your company. Visually, the Global Framework looks something like this: a container for your work shaped by these five main responsibilities around the perimeter.

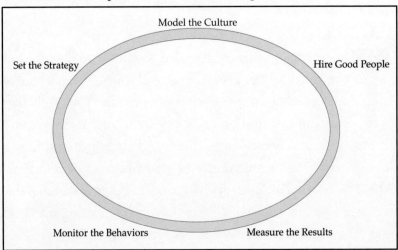

You may only think about the Global Framework a couple of times a year, even if you act on these categories much more frequently. You may only ask yourself a couple of times a year if you are doing a good job at these five things. Do you have the right people for the positions and the work that your team is doing now? Has the work changed at all, and do the people you have on the team still have the skills that are needed for the work you are doing currently? Do you have the right strategy based on the large market forces and the competition? Are you spending enough time with your employees to monitor their behaviors? Do you have the structure in place to know how you are doing? These kinds of questions are so broad that they tend to indicate only whether you are performing these activities well in the largest sense. If you are not doing one of these activities well, it usually requires a significant amount of time and tasks to get the category to the desired level. Realizing you don't have the best staff for several positions may take months to change. Realizing you are not accurately measuring the results of your staff may take months to correct.

Occasionally, I find I have the "ungrounded feeling" because I have not been thinking about my Global Framework. Most of the time, though, the Global Framework is so inherent to daily operations that we are supporting it even if we don't realize it. For example, the annual performance-review process addresses the "Hire Good People" component. If you are not measuring your team's results, your manager will likely ask you for your results. These five categories are so core to any company that they essentially happen naturally.

Your Primary Framework

I also used to get the ungrounded feeling when I was focusing exclusively on the near-term functionality of my role and responsibilities. For example, when running a region that included important customers, such as hospital systems, I would organize my thinking, time, and effort based on each hospital system. My digital "One Place" was based on these customers, my thinking was based on these customers, and most of my activities were planned through the lens of these customers. I organized my efforts around the question "What does this customer need for us to be successful?" This angle of approach is called the Primary Framework.

The Primary Framework is the next level down in hierarchy from the Global Framework and is a normal perspective from which to work.

> ***Something I have learned:*** *Most companies and leaders will naturally organize around the Primary Framework, as this framework is important to the near-term success of the team or department or the business.*

In my case, I framed my meetings, time, and effort around a customer-based model to ensure that all the activities of my staff were focused on meeting the needs of our customers. A leader who is responsible for running several internal departments might similarly have a Primary Framework around each department. Visually, this "lens" of thinking may look like the graphic below, in which each column represents a customer. The manager can organize his thinking about the categories of work based on the columns. Note that the Primary Framework exists within the Global Framework, as the primary supports the global.

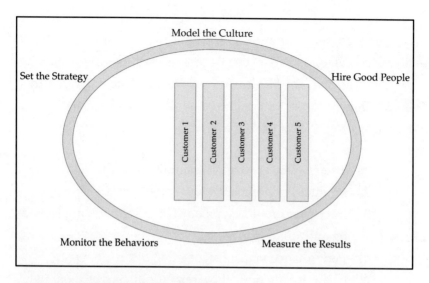

YOUR ALTERNATIVE FRAMEWORK

Although important, I believe that the Primary Framework is not actually the most effective plane from which to think, work, and operate. If this view is the only way you consider your organization, then you are missing the common areas that actually cut *across* the columns of the primary. There is a different and potentially lateral view to consider, which gives an even more holistic perspective of your role as a leader. This supplemental and complementary way to look at your organization is called the Alternative Framework. The Alternative Framework includes the focus areas that are common across or within your Primary Framework.

> **Something I have learned:** *While the Primary Framework focuses on the near-term needs of the business, the Alternative Framework focuses on the long term. It is the fertilizer that ensures a business's growth over time.*

To determine your Alternative Framework, you must seek to find the categories that cut across everything. As solutions president for Evolent Health (my role at the time of writing this book), my work in the Alternative Framework includes the following categories of job responsibility:

1. Talent (who is doing what and how well)
2. Product development (what we sell or do)
3. Infrastructure development (what we have in place to operate our department)
4. Performance management (how we are doing)
5. Client interactions (how our customers feel about us)

All five of these categories are relevant to every large customer under my responsibility. Each customer has a dependency on our company's talent, products, infrastructure, performance, and interactions with them, so an alternative way of thinking about the work I do for each customer is to look at the work I am doing across these categories as they apply to all customers.

Talent has traditionally been referred to as human resources. When I refer to talent, I am considering the professional development of my direct reports. Am I spending one-on-one time with each of my direct reports monthly? Am I observing the individuals doing their jobs and giving them feedback so when I am not there, they are a little bit better for me having observed them? Am I working with them to create development plans? Am I conducting quarterly check-ins? Am I planning hiring campaigns to support growth? All of these questions and activities go into the talent category of work. Talent is often and easily overlooked by leaders, as talent is not generally perceived as "what we do" as a company. Companies make and sell stuff or deliver services, so these aspects of the business are what managers generally think of, not the people.

Product development means coming up with new goods or services to sell to customers or improving the ones we currently sell to customers. This category includes activities such as research, development of new services or products, and pricing. Does our service match what the market wants? Does our price deliver value to the customer?

Infrastructure refers to investing time to make the company work better at creating or delivering our products or services. These activities include process improvements, vendor improvements, equipment improvements, and other similar improvements to the structural (generally internal) aspects of the business. What is creating internal problems or inefficiency, and how are we solving those problems and inefficiencies?

Performance management is described as monitoring how we are doing at creating or delivering our goods and services. This category is composed of metrics and dashboards and ways of understanding the core measurements of our product or service, both operationally and financially. Operational performance management examples are customers per store per day or client satisfaction per biometric-screening event or number of patients seen per nurse per week. Financial metrics are revenue, costs, and profit, all done in aggregate or as individual metrics.

Client interactions are self-explanatory. Getting out and talking to our customers. What are they saying? What are they *not* saying?

The examples provided are relevant to my current job and may not apply to your role. However, you can use my descriptions as a way to identify both your Primary and Alternative view of your work.

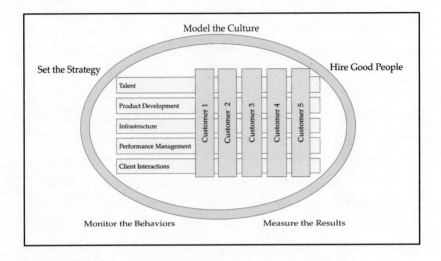

The visual above works for my current role but is not universal to all leaders. Some leaders may have only a subset of these categories, and some may have more than these categories. Leaders in other industries may have an entirely different Alternative Framework. For example, as a solution president I was responsible for product development, but as a market president I was not. As a market president, someone else created and refined our product or service and I just delivered it to the customer. Finding your Alternative Framework is unique to your job.

> **Something I have learned:** *If you arrange your thinking around an Alternative Framework, you can deliver more effective leadership support to your staff, your customers, and your company.*

Once you have established your Alternative Framework, you can begin to plan your time, effort, and output around this framework to effectively lead your team. I mean, *literally* organize your time, effort, and output around this framework. To ensure that I am thinking about talent, I plan four dedicated hours every month for talent. I actually block four hours and put the word "Talent" into the time block. I use this time to think generally if I am supporting my staff effectively, if I am on track for quarterly check-ins, if I am planning positions for future growth, and if I am getting out and doing observations of everyone. Without this Alternative Framework, I would likely never pull up out of the Primary (customer) Framework to think about talent as a body of work that needs cultivation and focus.

When I organize myself around the alternative, though, I develop initiatives and tasks that support each of these categories and benefit *all* customers. During one of these talent brainstorms, for example, I realized that our nurse managers had recently taken on a new type of work that was unfamiliar to them. We created a leadership-development program that trained the nurse managers on this new skill that was essential to their success. The training program benefited every customer because it generated better performance by every nurse. If I had only looked at one customer and one nurse manager, I may or may not have seen that lateral need across all customers.

Doing this same exercise around all five categories ensures I am looking at my role holistically and that my daily and weekly tasks take into account both the short-term needs and the long-term view. As I create action items, I am careful to assign them to one of the categories within my Alternative Framework. Then, looking at my digital One Place, I can quickly know if I am balanced across all five categories. If I don't have any tasks or initiatives in one of the categories, I can recognize the gap and allocate time in that category to ensure maximum success over the long term.

I feel incredibly grounded when I can look at my job through both the Primary and the Alternative Framework. I can sense that

Frazer Buntin

I am taking care of both the near-term needs as well as the longer-term needs. This dual confidence helps me tremendously because I know that a focus on the Primary Framework alone will create that feeling of not being prepared for the needs of the business six months from now, and a focus on the Alternative Framework alone will create disruption in the now with more fires to have to put out on a regular basis. As a leader, it is essential to approach work along both of these planes.

12
I FEEL LIKE MY TEAM IS UNGROUNDED

J ust as leaders can feel they are ungrounded, these same leaders can also feel that their team is ungrounded. This feeling typically comes from a gap that exists between the global mission of the company and the tactical work of the employees. That's why mission statements are so valuable for businesses. And yet, many of these mission statements end up hanging in a dusty frame in the lobby of the building and are only referenced by CEOs in town halls or all-employee emails. The result is that employees are disconnected from a larger sense of purpose. They lack a cohesive set of guiding principles that have practical application to their everyday work. These are principles that address the beliefs of the team, the parameters for how the team will work together, and the boundaries that the team will and will not tolerate. My experience has been that employees want these principles and guidelines. They want a common set of rules that everyone buys in to, so they have some degree of predictability for what is and isn't acceptable. Without these guidelines, people default to their own norms and perceptions, which vary across individuals. Feelings of mistrust, blame, and/or self-preservation then arise because there is no clear common ground. An ungrounded team can be very damaging to a business, while a grounded team can operate smoothly and effectively.

MONDAY-MORNING PRINCIPLES

I once led a team that was extremely ungrounded. In fact, it was comically dysfunctional when I took over. The group's previous manager had created a toxic culture of internal competition and distrust. He actually made the members of the sales team come into the office on Thanksgiving Day to practice their sales pitch in front of him. Incredible. No wonder the culture and principles of the team were a mess. Within my first two days on the job, the leader of every single department came to me and discreetly complained about every other department leader. They each said if so-and-so would do a better job, the company would be successful. Sales blamed IT. Marketing blamed finance. Operations blamed sales. Finance blamed everyone. Literally one person would open the door to leave my office and the person she had been talking about would walk in to talk about someone else. It was a revolving door of dysfunction. What I needed was for everyone to solve a lot of problems quickly, and to do so, we had to trust each other. I knew we would never get the company on track with the current culture, so I had to start over from scratch. We needed a set of principles for how we would operate individually and collectively that we could all agree on.

> **Something I have learned:** *The foundation of a grounded team lies in a set of practical core operating principles.*

Through a lot of trial and error, I have honed and refined a set of cultural guidelines, which I call "Monday-Morning Principles." These principles form the core values of our team: the things that we agree to, that we trust, value, and uphold. They are the underlying fabric of how we operate individually and together. They apply up and down and left to right so everyone works under the same set of guidelines and expectations. The Monday-Morning Principles include the following four standards of behavior:

1. Risk-free communication
2. Rapid rate of surfacing and solving problems
3. Following the process
4. Extreme customer responsiveness

These principles are local to my team, and I don't try to force them onto the broader company. However, it is my experience that other managers tend to latch on to these principles once they see them in action. I have also witnessed these principles move across a company in a grassroots manner because they work.

RISK-FREE COMMUNICATION

Risk-Free Communication (RFC) is probably the number-one

most effective enabler of group and business success that I have seen in my career. This principle is incredibly powerful when put to use in the correct way. Risk free assumes that we are all mature adults in business and that we must be able to communicate with each other in a way that has no risk. By risk free, I mean that individuals can ask questions and seek input without the risk of the recipient of those questions becoming defensive to the question or input. This requires immense trust. It takes trust to believe that you can raise a question or a concern and not expect defensiveness in return. This trust is secured through the formalization of the principle itself. When everyone has signed up for Risk-Free Communication as a way of working together, everyone can fall back on that agreement as a safety net. The lack of risk is two way, though. The other side of Risk-Free Communication means, as the recipient of the communication, you have to assume positive intent of the person who is coming to you with a question or seeking information. You have to trust the goodwill of that person without taking what they say personally. In essence, you have to separate your identity from the question or comment.

> **Something I have learned:** To separate your identity from a question or comment, you have to create some space between the question or statement and your response to it.

You create that space by believing in the intent of the questioner and perhaps even physically giving yourself some time before you respond to an email or get back to someone with an answer. Creating this space is very difficult and takes a lot of practice. Expect to fail, and when you do, apologize for violating the principle and try again the next time. The effort here is to respect, cultivate, and champion candor. Candor is the underlying goal, because without candor, a company doesn't really know what is going on. And if a company doesn't really know what is going on, that company will eventually get beaten by another company that does know what is going on. Once you really activate candor and Risk-Free Communication in your organization, your employees will experience the benefit of these practices, feel extremely connected to the principle, and develop a deep appreciation for the work environment.

A RAPID RATE OF SURFACING AND SOLVING PROBLEMS

A Rapid Rate of Surfacing and Solving Problems is the second most effective enabler. Businesses are full of problems. They lurk everywhere in every department, and some are old as crap and some are brand new. Problems span the full spectrum. They are small and easy to fix, and big and hard as hell to fix. Additionally, and incredibly, *all* the problems within a business are already known within the business at any given time. There are no unknown or hidden problems! Someone, somewhere within your company has likely seen or experienced every problem. She may not know it is a problem, or she may simply be tolerating the problem, but all of the problems are likely being experienced on a routine basis by at least one of the company's employees. Think about this for a minute. If you have an objective to be a perfectly run company, your organization already has the collective knowledge to achieve perfection.

Of course, perfection is unattainable because companies are evolving organizations, and with each microevolution comes more problems. Moreover, solving problems requires time and money, and problem solving should have a return on investment. Some problems have a big return on investment, some a very small return on investment, some no return on investment, and some a negative return on investment. Businesses spend a lot of time prioritizing which problems to solve. However, the vast majority of companies don't ever get close to knowing all the problems that should be "on the list" for solving. If you can improve the rate at which a company surfaces and solves problems, the prioritization process is more efficient, and many more problems can be solved.

The way to increase your Rate of Surfacing and Solving Problems is to enable a culture or principle of candor through Risk-Free Communication. Everyone needs to feel not only empowered to—but actually responsible for—bringing candor through RFC to talk about what is working and what is not working within the business. Everyone means everyone. If the lowest job–level person on the team feels that something isn't working and wants to bring it to the leader of that team, he needs to feel completely empowered to email "the boss" and tell her something sucks. The employee cannot have any fear of retribution for shining a light on a problem. If you can institute this type of culture into your company's DNA, you will create an army of problem solvers that will massively accelerate your Rate of Surfacing and Solving Problems and you will kick the crap out of your competition. What's more, your staff will love working for your company because they will feel heard and connected to the solutions that drive success.

I have heard people attempt to counter this concept by claiming that RFC or candor will just create a culture of complaining. Without a complementary culture of rapidly *solving* problems, this statement can be true. Each employee must have an obligation to bring a potential solution when raising an issue or problem. This does not mean every problem will be solved, though. If the team or a leader acknowledges the problem yet decides through analysis that their return on the investment of solving that problem is not high enough to make the list for now, the problem may be deemed as acceptable. Regardless, everyone has bought into the process of Surfacing and Solving Problems and is more likely to be okay tolerating any problems that are not fixed right away.

The principle of Surfacing and Solving Problems is very liberating and empowering for employees. Staff members can feel a sense of recognition and accomplishment by simply pointing out something that is not working and trying to help fix it. Embracing and celebrating the activity of surfacing problems gets employees excited to get into problem-solving mode. This principle can change the entire feeling of a team, as the individuals feel empowered to do something about the problems of their job.

FOLLOW THE PROCESS

A third principle is to Follow the Process. Businesses are complex organizations full of variability if left unattended. Variability creates cost, especially when employees spin their wheels trying to "figure out" the same microactivities. Repeated attempts to figure out how to do something are a huge waste of time. When all of this wasted time is added together, it creates significant cost, usually in the form of unnecessary staff. In fact, anytime someone comes to me and asks to hire an additional person to do the same type of work others are doing, I always consider if we need to develop processes for a particular business function that will give us more efficiency versus hiring another person to do the same work in an inefficient manner. When a group of employees actually stops doing the work and thinks about the work itself and how to make it more efficient, the output is a business process that has the collective input of the group trying to solve the problem. This investment of time typically yields a significant return of time, as that same group has pooled all their best practices. The best practices then become a business process for the members of the group to follow the next time they do that same task or piece of work.

There are all kinds of ways to document business processes, from flow charts to Word documents. However, having an operating culture of following the process once it has been defined can be an effective way to reduce variability (and therefore cost) and improve execution.

> **Something I have learned:** *Developing and operating a process-based culture is not enough on its own, because every process will become irrelevant and begin to fail over time.*

It is essential to combine Risk-Free Communication with a Rapid Rate of Surfacing and Solving Problems to develop a process-based principle. Employees generally want to know how something should work. They also tend to despise wasted work. Having a process-based culture will help your staff feel grounded.

EXTREME CUSTOMER RESPONSIVENESS

The last Monday-Morning Principle is Extreme Customer Responsiveness. Every business has customers. Some companies have individuals as customers, and some have other businesses as customers. Inevitably, every business will fail its customers. Businesses will fail to give their customers the products and services they have committed to in small ways and sometimes very large ways. These failures happen all the time, as businesses are complex organizations. Most business-to-business companies have fewer customers than business-to-consumer companies. If a company has fewer customers, each one is extremely valuable to the company's existence and success. When you fail your customers, especially in a business-to-business environment, you feel like crap. You also feel scared. Scared you are going to be blamed or perhaps even fired.

It used to be that retail companies could fail their customers and there were few large-scale consequences of the failure because there was no way for the customer to share the failure with other customers at scale. Perhaps the customer of a retail store who purchased an item that broke the next day could stand outside the store with a sign saying how the store sold them a broken item. If the company had nine thousand stores, one person standing outside one store for one day wouldn't lead to any significant change within the company that sold the broken item. However, with the growth of online, consumer-driven feedback mechanisms, such as Yelp or feedback stars, consumers now have an incredible scale to voice a company's failures. As such, all companies now are susceptible to the implications of their failures, and so responding to these failures in a meaningful way when they occur is critical to business success.

I love Extreme Customer Responsiveness to failure. No one expects someone who fails them to own it. No one expects someone who fails them to tell them the truth. People generally expect others to be defensive, even when a failure is clear. Extreme Customer Responsiveness is the opposite. It means going absolutely to the far ends of transparency, communication, and correction with the customer when you fail. These moments are a chance to blow your customer's expectations away with your response to your own failure.

> **Something I have learned:** You and your employees
> need to feel incredibly empowered to correct a failure for your
> customers.

The first step is to own the failure with rapid communication. As soon as you discover you have failed a customer, you need to contact that customer as quickly as possible, take responsibility for what happened, and let them vent. You also need to inform them of your specific communication plan as you seek resolution to the problem. Tell them when they can expect to hear back from you.

The second step is to be extremely honest and transparent with your customers as to what happened and what you plan to do about it. Let them behind the curtain into your company and your processes and explain to them in detail where it failed and why. For example, recall the phlebotomist example from Healthways where none of the examiners showed up at the ball-bearing plant. I actually explained our entire process to the customer of how we selected, screened, and reserved the phlebotomists. I walked them through our entire internal process of logistics for preparing for one of the events. I explained with full transparency the risks associated with our process and the financial trade-offs we made with our pricing for those risks. I explained all the steps we built into the model to confirm and reconfirm the wellness event. I had to give them full transparency into the potential points of failure of our service, so they understood the inherent risk of the service itself and all the ways we had mitigated the risk. The client needed to understand our process deeply to regain trust in us. Every time I did this transparency activity with a client, the client ended up respecting the lengths to which we would go in our process discipline.

The third step is to think of ways to exceed the expectations of your customer. This step is an area where you can get creative and even challenge yourself to do more than you did the last time you had to engage in ECR. I have sent a lot of handwritten notes and flowers to customers, patients, and others over the years in an effort to get creative with Extreme Customer Responsiveness.

An additional benefit to Extreme Customer Responsiveness is that your employees will appreciate having a framework for managing these situations and the autonomy to correct them. They will appreciate not having to try to hide behind problems and mistakes and will embrace this principle.

PRINCIPLES AS A SUSTAINABLE COMPETITIVE ADVANTAGE

These four principles, when developed together, will create an absolute Sustainable Competitive Advantage. If you can use Risk-Free Communication to Rapidly Surface and Solve Problems and then create repeatable business processes with Extreme Customer Responsiveness, you can create and deliver products and services more effectively than your competitors. Your company can have a lower cost basis, have smoother operations, have fewer technology issues, implement faster, create a better user experience, and/or do whatever you do generally better than anyone else. The advantage, in this case, is a *cultural* sustainable competitive edge. Very few companies think of company culture as an avenue for a competitive advantage. Normally, competitive advantages come from lower cost or intellectual property or size and scale. A *cultural* competitive advantage is much more difficult to create but also has the potential to be much more difficult to replicate. If a company can activate a competitive advantage through culture, it can receive a tremendous return on the time invested in that advantage, reaping long-term benefits for the team and the company.

> **Something I have learned:** It is up to you to determine the principles that apply to your job, work team, or department.

The four Monday-Morning Principles I have outlined are not universal—they are simply ones that I have found to be fairly portable from one job to another, one company to another, and one industry to another. What works for your job, your team, and your department will be different. You need to determine what those guiding principles should be. No matter what you decide, having these types of practical operating principles will help your team feel grounded, as it will be clear to everyone what is important and how to operate on a daily basis.

I'll start with a bit of level-setting—what exactly is a Monday-Morning Principle? This one is extremely simple: "principles or tactics that you can use when you show up to work on a Monday morning." When I began my transition path from healthcare strategy consultant to healthcare business operator, I had no idea how helpful these would become. As a consultant, my job was to solve problems and dispense advice on challenging topics. For the most part these solutions and advice stopped well short of clearly defining "What does this mean for me on a Monday morning?" and had me handing off to someone else for execution. As a business leader, managing a P&L and largely creating value through the work of my teams, the currency of the realm quickly shifted from ideas to actions. To be successful, I needed to create an environment where individual members knew what they needed to get done, and to maintain any semblance of work-life balance, I needed to do that in a way that didn't require my involvement with every step. This led me to two types of Monday-Morning Principles—the first related to how I managed my teams and the second to how I managed my own contributions and time.

Monday-Morning "Team" Principles:

1. *Transfer Context:* For individuals to perform autonomously and at their best, they need context. Without it they inevitably come back with questions about what they should do. A highly productive week for the team begins Monday morning with sharing of context so that they understand the "why" that allows them to make their own decisions about the "what" of their work.

2. *Risk-Free Communication:* In a complicated environment, time spent worrying about consequences rather than surfacing problems is time wasted that could be spent on something productive. An environment where individuals can raise their hand to flag issues without worrying about blame or punishment is a critical foundation for a high-performing team. This is an easy thing to say, but a hard thing to do.

3. *Rate of Surfacing and Solving Problems:* In my line of work (transforming healthcare), obstacles and challenges are inevitable—it's not a matter of if something will go wrong, but rather when. Instead of seeing this as a negative, it's important for all members of the team to see a problem as an opportunity to generate a solution and in the process build deeper trust with the customer. If you're going to embrace Risk-Free Communications, you should expect to encounter some problems that need to be solved.

Monday-Morning Principles for Me:

1. *Define and Follow a Process: This one was hard for me—I'm by nature uncomfortable with a lot of structure—but I found that committing to a defined process to manage my team and prioritize my own work actually created more flexibility for me. Some examples of this were (1) weekly check-ins, with my direct reports organized around their most important responsibilities with clear metrics to define success, including a consistent template and data wherever possible, (2) time spent at the end of each day to pull up and define the most important activities and outcomes for the following day—with time blocked to accomplish these, and (3) intentional planning around tactical and strategic work—both of these are critical, and without careful planning it's easy to spend 100 percent of your time in the weeds.*

2. *Relentless Delegation: This one is still a work in progress, as I really enjoy rolling up my sleeves and digging in to solve the problem. However, it's been important to recognize what I am uniquely positioned to contribute and to work to focus as much of my time on those activities as possible. Ironically, in many cases, these free up time for me and provide additional satisfaction to the delegate.*

—Scott P., *Senior Vice President of Operations*

13
I STILL DON'T FEEL SUCCESSFUL

This is a book about feelings, but it is also a book about action. What is the purpose of all of these tactics and philosophies? What is the purpose of work in the first place? Why do we care about understanding and improving ourselves? Why do we want to experience success? Why do we need to feel passion?

All of the methods in this book have the potential to accelerate your professional success. Success, though, is extremely difficult to define. Several hours into a twelve-hour trail-running event with a running friend, we were asking each other questions to pass the time and he asked me who I thought was successful. I honestly could not answer the question, because I don't think of specific people in terms of success. I think of people in terms of defining characteristics, such as funny or intelligent or outgoing. I may think of them as successful in business, but I have no idea if they are successful in parenting or well-being or as a spouse or a friend. We can't really see others holistically enough to determine whether they are a "success." Over time, you may find that success in your professional career is defined much more broadly than you imagined. Success becomes more than title or compensation. Success becomes something much more abstract, and just as you reach some achievement milestone, your definition of success shifts or evolves. What does this tell us? I suggest being very careful with that word and especially with that label. Success is something that can be understood as opposed to something that can be "achieved," because there is no finish line. My hope is that you can use the principles outlined in this book to help you not only *strive to* achieve success but help you *understand* what success means to you personally. You may find that seeking to understand what success means to you is actually the core part of the experience of your professional life.

PURPOSE AND MEANING

At a very basic level, we work to feed and shelter ourselves and our families. Accomplishing those objectives, we have more freedom than we think to determine what kind of work we want to do and why. I challenge you to place "Purpose and Meaning" at the top of your requirement for your next job.

> **Something I have learned:** *Purpose and Meaning don't have to be altruistic, but rather have to be authentic.*

Finding Purpose and Meaning will be specific to you, your interests, and your talents. I love Venn diagrams because the intersection of circles is where interesting stuff happens. Imagine the following Venn diagram. On one side is Intense Personal Reflection, which we talked about in the first chapter.

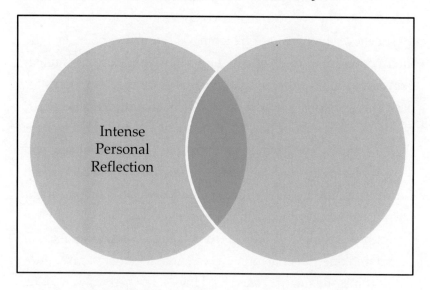

On the other side is "Don't Give a Shit." Yes, that is correct. Don't give a shit.

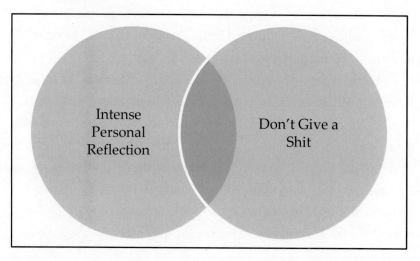

For about fifteen years, I only used the left side. Left to my own wiring and tendencies, I reflect intensely pretty much nonstop. In fact, I have a thinking obsession. Perhaps even a thinking addiction. I am in sort of a personal recovery for this condition. Likely many of you reading this book have the same condition, though you may not even realize you have it.

I believe humans are reaching a breaking point at the intersection of the simplicity and the complexity of human existence. I have a theory that, originally, we used our brains for basic survival skills. We won the food-chain battle because of our brains. We figured out how to get food, water, and shelter better than everything else because we were able to think, evaluate, and solve problems for survival. Here's a rough example: Back when we were running around in loincloths and living in caves, we might have used our cognitive skills to feed ourselves. We would have analyzed the plants and animals to maximize our food intake. All of this thinking and analyzing was essential to our existence. If we didn't think and analyze, we died. However, when we were done using our brain to analyze and determine ways to feed ourselves, we turned it off. We used our brain as a tool, and then we "put it down" when we were done with it, just as we would put down a hammer when we were finished hitting nails. In essence, when we no longer needed to think, we stopped thinking.

In modern times, however, we don't need our brains for basic survival anymore at all. I can turn a knob and get water. I can turn another knob and get fire. I can go to a store and I don't have to figure out how to kill the groceries to eat them. Survival is a brainless activity. We actually don't have to think to survive.

And yet, the complexity of our current lives is potentially beyond the capability of our brains to adapt and cope with it. Our brains are not equipped to handle the pace of parenting, technology, information, options, choices, stimuli, and feelings. So, what do we do? We tend to live mentally in the past or, more often, in the future. We see today as an obstacle to the future, which holds some salvation. The future will bring us that job we want, that financial security we want, that recognition we want, that house we want, that freedom we want. Our fears and wants, and we all have them, eat the present to feed the future. Today doesn't matter to our fears and wants. Today is something to be harvested to attain the future. Today is just a way of doing something to get what we want in the future, when everything will be okay. When we will be happy. When we will be fulfilled. When we will have peace.

This is crap. This is bullshit. But for years I was consumed with this way of thinking. My story is that for about fifteen years, I *never* stopped thinking.

Ever.

Within two seconds of waking up *every* morning, I was thinking about something in the future. Work, house, travel, weekend. I would take a shower and not remember anything about it. Whether I washed my hair, how the water felt, nothing. I would be totally absent getting dressed, fixing breakfast with my wife, talking to my kids, driving to work.

Everything was absent.

Even though I was there, I missed everything.

Here is the deal, though. I was *really* good at it. I mastered it. I could be laughing with my wife and kids at breakfast and not really be there. I could drive down the road and not really be there. I could sit in meetings and participate actively and intelligently and not really be there. The *only* time I was present was either after about three beers or if I was climbing up some steep mountain or racing down giant rapids in a river. My thinking obsession was stealing everything from me, though I didn't realize it. Occasionally, I felt the anxiety of the background noise, but I could not see that the state of mind I was living in was the thing creating the background noise.

Everything was the future.

The problem is when you live this way, you are never content. You are never happy. And most of all, you are always scared and always wanting. Fear and wanting are the drivers of this thinking obsession. Fear of not becoming something your ego is telling you that you need to become. Wanting something to bring you happiness, to make your moment complete, your life complete. A genius of understanding the human condition, Eckhart Tolle, kindly tells us in his book *The Power of Now* that the future is just a bunch of moments that haven't occurred yet.

This is it, though. Right now is all we have.

THE GRAY SPACE

Here is the irony in this topic. Almost anytime I talk to someone about this topic, they say something about wanting to be more present with their kids, and then they pull out their phone and show me some phone app that is supposed to be their salvation to living. This is not about your kids or your spouses or your friends. This isn't about an app, either. It is about you.

I can't give you the answers for you. I only can share some tactics that work for me. The gray space in the middle of the Venn diagram is where you need to be. The space between Intense Personal Reflection and Don't Give a Shit is the holy land. This gray space is the place to think and plan and evaluate yourself and your life. The gray space is where you will discover what success means for you *at that time*. The gray space is where you will face down your fears and your wants.

The gray space is also where, once you have done those activities, *you put that shit down.*

You lay your brain and your thinking down on the desk, and you go take a shower and feel the water on your face. You go have breakfast with your family and you listen with an empty mind to what they are saying, and you look them in the eyes and feel yourself taking in their words. Soaking in their words and their expressions and their feelings.

You drive to work and actually look around at what you see, and you feel the steering wheel in your hands.

You sit in meetings and engage with passion and intelligence and vigor *only* for the topic at hand.

This is your life. This is success.

THIS!

You are successful right now! You are doing the right things right now for your life, so bust your ass and then give your ass a break.

This is really damn hard. It is a daily practice. It is a discipline. You will have times when you backslide and you fail and you need to regroup and keep trying. You will be consumed with some idea or desire for something in the future. Something to bring you happiness. So, do some Intense Personal Reflection—or whatever the hell you want to call it—to hit the release valve and then shut that shit down. Your practice is a path, and if you grasp that the gray space exists, then just being in the gray space can be a path that is rewarding in itself.

What do you get with this belief or awareness or understanding?

Something I have learned: *We can have a deep appreciation for life in aggregate through a deep appreciation for life in segments.*

Just as your career isn't one big thing but a series of countless segments, so too is your *life*. Again from Mr. Tolle, in experiencing fully these segments—or moments—our reward is stillness. With stillness comes peace. With peace comes joy and with joy comes love. Not necessarily love as in "I love you," but love as in deep gratitude. Gratitude for the extremely subtle moment that a big work initiative quietly turns a corner and starts to be effective. Gratitude for playing a game of Uno with your eight-year-old daughter and seeing the joy on her face as she throws down a Wild Card on you to win the game. Gratitude for standing in a field at sunrise with your dog and looking up as the last stars fade with the rising sunlight of dawn. Gratitude for your wife reaching over to hold your hand under the covers as you turn out the light.

This is success. This is what you get.

Go get it.

CHEAT SHEET

(some people call this an index)

Of course, I think you should read the book in its entirety because it's important to understand context before you go about applying practical tactics, but if you need a cheat sheet, here it is.

Frazer Buntin

You want to know how to set the strategy . . . Chapter 10
You want to know how to measure results . . . Chapter 10
You want to know how to deal with a boss who sucks . . . Chapter 9
You want to know how to manage your manager . . . Chapter 9
You want to know how to find some peace . . . Chapter 13

GLOSSARY OF TERMS

Alternative Framework: A different midterm perspective on the work that you do

Ass-Boss: Someone you don't want to be but probably will encounter

Common Thread: The similarity of experience that has occurred throughout your career

Degree of Stretch: A measurement of how difficult your job is for you

Funnel: A general description of how your career will happen

Funnel Stem: The point at which your job generally feels natural

Global Framework: The most abstract and highest level of thinking about the work that you do

Intense Personal Reflection: The only way you can influence your path through the Funnel

Line of Boredom: The point at which your job no longer challenges you

Line of Maximum Capability: The point at which your job challenges you beyond your capability

Monday-Morning Principles: Practical guidelines for you and your team

Oh Shit Moments: Moments you can expect to have and are responsible for fixing

One Place: A digital place to host all of your nonrecurring work

Primary Framework: The most apparent way of thinking about the work that you do

Process of Selection and Elimination: Thinking about what you like and don't like about your job

Rate of Surfacing and Solving Problems: The pace at which you or your team course-corrects the business

Risk-Free Communication: Saying what is on your mind without fear of retribution

Skit: A highly rehearsed speech you give in a job interview

ACKNOWLEDGMENTS

Thank you to Julianne Crims, who came to a simple, small Q&A session I did years ago and sent me the email that nudged me to put my experiences into this book.

Thank you to Raina Avalon, who opened my eyes and curiosity to the world of professional development. She gave me books, encouraged me to go to seminars, and taught me the first steps of being a people manager.

Thanks to Jeff Owen, who taught me how to find more capacity within people than I could have ever imagined. The many miles Jeff and I traveled together across small towns taught me the value in preparation and the benefits of discomfort in coaching others. Lastly, thanks to Jeff for challenging me to go big with presentations, including a rotating stage, artificial-smoke machines, and strobe lights to introduce a simple metal container that likely changed my career forever.

Thanks to Kathleen Guion for the incredible lesson of "celebrate the relative but measure the absolute." Thanks also to Kathleen for taking someone in charge of highly consumable merchandising and putting him in charge of a "feature merchandising" project. The project was one of the main springboards for my career.

Thanks to Chris Hilton for being an incredibly confident wingman and always being up for building and fixing the business. He was the yin for my yang, and I have a lot of yang.

Thanks to Lucius Burch for going in first with his capital. Thanks to all the folks at Nashville Capital Network, Heritage Group, FCA, and other angels for supporting me through the tough times and the tougher times.

Thanks to Mike O'Neil for referring the Evolent folks to me, which resulted in all the rewarding work there. Thanks to the leadership team and all the Evolenteers for pulling alongside me to change the way healthcare is delivered in our nation.

Thanks to my sister, Varina, for her editing work and putting a keen eye to my not-so-keen writing. Thanks to my brother, Jeffrey, for being there to share and reflect on professional war stories.

Thanks to my mom and dad for raising me with a silver spoon in one hand and a brown shovel in the other. The combination of your love and support with our unique environment cultivated my entire path. None of my success would have happened without you both.

Thank you to my wonderful kids, James and Neely. Your hugs carried me through the travel, and your sincere way of asking "How was *your* day, Dad?" always melted my heart.

And finally, and mostly, thank you to my amazing wife, Tiffany. You have been there when I needed to vent, when I needed to travel, and when I needed to listen. You are so grounded, and you are my anchor to love. I carry your heart, and I will be forever grateful that you carry mine.

CONTACT ME

In the beginning of this book, under the title of the Preface, I suggested that you let me know if this material was helpful. If you want to give me feedback of any kind or just want to share a story or anecdote, email me at fbuntin@monkeyfeelings.com. I look forward to hearing from you.

ABOUT THE AUTHOR

Frazer Buntin is a healthcare executive, entrepreneur, and student of human emotion as it relates to work. His career has spanned from being a buyer of toilet paper all the way to leading companies as a CEO. He has won absolutely no awards for his writing, but then again, this is his first book. Frazer lives in Nashville, Tennessee, and enjoys spending time with his family, paddle-boarding rivers, and trail running. Rather than use a traditional headshot photo for this book, he chose this picture of him during the Zion Traverse because it was an epic day that he wants to share with you.